THE BUSY MUM'S VEGETARIAN COOKBOOK

THE BUSY MUM'S VEGETARIAN COOKBOOK

Family mealtimes made easy with 120 delicious meat-free recipes

Mary Gwynn

SIMON &
SCHUSTER
ILLUSTRATED

London · New York · Sydney · Toronto · New Delhi

A CBS COMPANY

First published in Great Britain by
Simon & Schuster UK Ltd, 2013
A CBS COMPANY

10 9 8 7 6 5 4 3 2 1

SIMON & SCHUSTER
ILLUSTRATED BOOKS
Simon & Schuster UK Ltd
222 Gray's Inn Road
London
WC1X 8HB

www.simonandschuster.co.uk

Simon & Schuster Australia
Sydney

Simon & Schuster India
New Delhi

Commercial director: Ami Richards
Project editor: Sharon Amos
Designer: Meg Georgeson
Photography: David Merewether
Stylist: Cherry Whytock
Production manager: Katherine Thornton
Art director: Corinna Farrow
Managing editor: Lorraine Jerram

A CIP catalogue record for this book is
available from the British Library

ISBN 978-0-85720-595-7

Colour reproduction by Dot Gradations Ltd
Printed and bound in China

Huge thanks

As you can probably tell on reading through the pages, this book comes with the input of so many wonderful people – family, friends and colleagues. I've been lucky enough to work with the same talented team who made my previous Busy Mum's book such a pleasure to produce, so thank you again to the ever-patient David Merewether, who took the photos, and stylist Cherry Whytock, who brought her wonderful vision of colour to the mix without compromising the food. And to daughter Isobel for following in her sister Lucy's footsteps as a cheerful and hard-working assistant throughout the weeks of photography (and we managed to throw her a big 21st birthday party right in the middle of it!).

The team at Simon & Schuster have been particularly understanding and supportive, as this book has been produced while I've been dealing with family illness. Their flexibility and calm acceptance of changed deadlines have ensured the project has never faltered and helped me produce a book that looks and reads as we had all hoped. Sharon Amos has worked her magic on the copy, and Meg Georgeson has designed once more pages of colour and freshness that really do justice to the food.

My family have been particularly important over the last year or so of writing, cooking and photographing for this book. So thanks to daughters, sisters, nephew and nieces. But most of all this is dedicated to my parents, who supported and believed in me but, above all, gave me my love of food shared with others, a wonderful way of bringing people together. They won't see this book but it wouldn't have been produced without them both. My love and gratitude go to them.

Praise for *The Busy Mum's Cookbook*

'This brilliant book has given me the inspiration to cook tasty, nutritious meals using local ingredients while I am busy leading a hectic life. Most of the ingredients are readily available and I don't need to plan too far ahead. Thank you, Mary, for inspiring me – a definite must for all those busy people who love food but don't have time to slave over a hot stove.'

'This is the cookery book I've been waiting for. It's full of really easy-to-understand and easy-to-make, delicious recipes that everyone will enjoy. It's really practical and down to earth – you can tell it's been written for real people with real lives. And every page makes you think yummmm! If you only use one cookery book, this should be the one.'

'A brilliant cookery book for mums who want to cook no-nonsense recipes for the family, but who still really care about food ... here are tons of recipes that use only economical, seasonal ingredients. I will be using this book a lot!'

'This is by far the best cookbook I own. All of the recipes are quick, easy and taste fantastic. And they are very family friendly, but would also appeal to those who aren't busy – or a mum!'

'Lordy, I could go on talking about my favourite recipes from this book for hours. This book is PERFECT for students.'

'Or busy dads, for that matter. Practical, no-nonsense recipes, laid out nicely in an easy-to-read and -follow manner.'

'A really useful and good-looking book, which is going to get well used in my kitchen.'

'Mary Gwynn's book gives good practical advice, not just for busy mums but for all of us who like to cook but do not have much time.'

'I am always on the go, helping to look after three grandchildren. I found this cookery book great and easy to follow. The variety and choice is brilliant and I refer to it all the time.'

'As soon as *The Busy Mum's Cookbook* arrived through the post I got cracking ... we've been feasting on fantastic dishes for days now. What a recipe book!'

'The kids have nearly all had clear plates each time I've used the recipes from this book – a must-have for people with busy lifestyles who still want to cook in the kitchen!'

'*The Busy Mum's Cookbook* belongs on everyone's shelf ... not only are the recipes easy and cost efficient but they are also utterly delicious. The chapter on meals that magic into packed lunches has reformed my working week ... This book hasn't been in my life for very long but I'm not sure how I ever got by without it ... a cookbook which will inspire even the most reluctant chef to bin the frozen food.'

A selection of Amazon reviews

contents

busy mum's know-how

As a cook, I have learnt from experience that the term 'vegetarian' means different things to different people, which can make catering for mixed groups of family and friends a little daunting. To us busy mums, it's yet another complication to add to the challenge of feeding the family. My sister Jane has a saying, 'the family that eats together stays together', and I know she is right.

But these days managing to get the family in one place at all is a challenge in itself – and then coming up with a meal that everyone can (or will) eat would stretch any well-equipped chef's establishment, let alone a busy mum with little time and limited budget. Throw a veggie or two into the mix, and the whole thing can seem too much altogether, making it all too easy to give up the ghost and serve up something different for each person, turning to convenience food and the microwave.

But help is at hand: there is an alternative. My clever recipes can easily be adapted to cater for all tastes so that everyone can sit down together and enjoy the same dishes with just minor variations on the plate.

Where do I start?

My first piece of advice to you is to forget the old model of 'meat and two veg', and completely change the focus of meals. One of the joys of eating in this country is the way we soak up lots of influences for our food – many of the cuisines we have embraced are based on vegetarian dishes, usually for reasons of economics. So think of a wonderful spread of tapas, mezze, curries, or even a Scandinavian breakfast table, and take inspiration from there. Make one large dish, such as a curry or vegetable gratin, the centrepiece of your meal, and add lots of side offerings. In this way meat eaters can be catered for by having a side dish of grilled chicken or sausages to add to their plate, vegetarians who aren't vegans can choose from mozzarella or Cheddar … you get the idea! Or at some point in the recipe I'll suggest that you can separate a dish into two batches and add meat or fish to one to satisfy the non-veggies in your family. My ex-sister-in-law had the challenge of catering for two children at opposing ends of the food spectrum: one who was strictly vegetarian and the other who ate only meat. She really struggled when it came to cooking a shared meal and it was with her in mind that I came up with these recipes, designing them with built-in flexibility.

So I have written this book from the cook's perspective – she/he is the one trying to create a single meal that the whole family can enjoy together. Most importantly, the recipes fit the aim I set out when I first edited a vegetarian food magazine for the BBC – they must all taste good. They have only made it into this book if they get the 'delicious' vote from all who have tried them – vegetarians or meat eaters. No flavour compromises have been made because of the lack of meat; likewise there is nothing here pretending to be meat but not tasting as good.

I make no apologies if this sounds like the veggies are getting all the attention; the non-veggies could all do with eating a little less meat and I guarantee that even confirmed carnivores will be coming back for second helpings.

My main criteria for the dishes I've included are as follows. They should be:
- healthy and well balanced
- budget-conscious
- quick to prepare (or slow to cook with little preparation)
- something everyone can eat together

Why eat together?

Preparing and sharing food is a vital form of social glue — it brings people together, providing an opportunity for many of what I consider life's most important lessons: how to manage cutlery and talk to the people around you without spitting or mumbling; how to deal with the discomfort or boredom of sitting still for a period of time; and how to eat what is put in front of you without negative comment. Lonely meals on trays in front of a screen do none of these. And I think we are only just starting to realise how vital these skills are for success in the wider world, and what we are risking by raising a generation whose main influences seem to come through some kind of monitor or electronic device. Whatever the papers or government say, these are not things that they teach at school, and social skills are more important than ever. We are only just starting to understand what we are in danger of losing, and our children are the ones who will suffer the consequences.

What type of veggie are you?

Eating less meat is increasingly becoming a fact of modern life. The key reasons for turning to a meat-free diet fit into four main areas — ethical, economic, health and personal taste — and that will dictate to what extent people become vegetarian. Many of us are conscious of several of these factors and may have to take others into account as we go through life.

As a cook my advice is don't get hung up on 'why'. Instead, concentrate on 'what'. It is vital that you know exactly what the term means to the people you are cooking for — it's very upsetting for someone to eat something hidden that they object to or are allergic to.

When I started planning this book my editor asked me to define the main types of vegetarian and maybe attempt to come up with a name for each. I found it an impossible task – trying just made me realise that there are as many types, or maybe as many different reasons, for giving up meat as there are people doing so. And it's such a personal decision that can have a great variety of triggers, which is why I believe it is wrong to stigmatise anyone for choosing what he/she will and won't eat.

The recipes you will find in these pages are all vegetarian as defined by the criteria of the Vegetarian Society: they do not contain meat products of any kind, no poultry, fish or shellfish, but with one exception – I have compromised on vegetarian cheeses. As I am not strictly veggie myself, I have used non-vegetarian cheeses made with rennet (which comes from a cow's stomach) for the recipes. Vegetarian cheeses are made with a rennet alternative, though many artisan cheese makers consider them inferior. But if cooking for strict veggies, please substitute vegetarian alternatives in the recipes. You can find quite a wide selection, from feta to mozzarella to Cheddar and even Camembert – be sure to look out for the V symbol on the packaging.

Planning ahead

There is no getting away from the fact that cooking without meat involves more thinking and planning. Meat is such a useful ingredient for providing easy-access nutrients, but we now know that too much has a downside from a health and environmental perspective. I have made the decision to eat only locally produced meat and fish on an occasional basis. So I plan accordingly to ensure that I have plenty of ingredients in my store cupboard and fridge that make cooking for my family as simple and time-friendly as possible, while maintaining good nutrition – and not forgetting taste, of course!

When you are excluding any major food group for whatever reason, I suggest you do your nutrition homework and make sure you understand the basics of eating a healthy diet – actually, I recommend you do this whatever you eat. People criticise vegetarians for being unhealthy by excluding meat but modern omnivores are not necessarily food saints themselves. If you're looking online, do go to a reputable source of information, as there is so much confusing advice available (try the Vegetarian Society's website, www.vegsoc.org/).

Small children and a vegetarian diet

I have not included specific recipes for the under-fives in this book, although I know they will enjoy many of the dishes on these pages. This is because I am not a nutritionist by training, and I believe that you need a good understanding of the needs of growing children before taking the decision to exclude any food group from their diet. But that's not to say that a healthy vegetarian diet is completely unsuitable for small children: the Vegetarian Society recommends that it's ideal for everyone when properly managed.

However, I know that as a mum and cook, growing children need the right balance of nutrients at every stage of development. Feeding them a diet based on wholefoods and low-fat ingredients that is suitable for an adult can deprive small children of the building blocks they need to develop. So if, after a school visit to a farm, your four-year-old suddenly announces he or she is giving up meat, I really recommend you do more research.

Having said that, all parents worry at some time about what their children are, or aren't, eating. My nephew James was a fussy eater from the word go and seemingly lived on milk and digestive biscuits for the first two years of his life. My poor sister despaired of him but he is now a strapping 25-year-old. So don't worry too much. With an understanding of the basis of a good diet, you can subtly guide things in the right direction.

What exactly am I eating?

One of the advantages of home-cooked vegetarian food is you know exactly what has gone into it – or maybe that should be what hasn't! When buying readymade products, vegetarians need to become adept at reading labels and spotting hidden ingredients that sometimes pop up in the most unexpected places. As a cook I know to avoid using gelatine (made from cattle bones) to set mousses but I still managed to forget that it gets used in sweets such as the marshmallows I made a mistake with in my recipe for chunky chocolate biscuit cake on page 178. (I've left the marshmallows in the photo as a reminder to you all of how easy it is to come unstuck! The recipe works just as well without them.)

Chocolate lovers need to check for whey powder, which is a by-product of cheese making, and rennet will have been used in the process. It can also be found in crisps, cakes and biscuits. The other pitfall for the cook is ingredients such as Worcestershire sauce and Thai curry pastes – the former contains anchovy while the latter relies on shrimp paste. Check the labels and look out for vegetarian versions. And watch out for meat and chicken stocks used in vegetable soups. Go to the Vegetarian Society website for more detailed lists of what to avoid (www.vegsoc.org/).

The essential ingredients

The basic food groups for a healthy vegetarian diet are as follows. Make sure you include all of them in your store cupboard and on your shopping list.

Fruit and veg

These should make up at least a third of what is on your plate – you shouldn't have a problem with managing at least the recommended five a day that way. Think stir fries, veg stews and soups, big salads.

(I found the way to get my children to eat salad was to serve it with plenty of delicious dressing.) Since fruit and veg come in all shapes, sizes and shades, it's easy to serve a rainbow of colours – that way, you know you're maximising vitamins and minerals.

I really try to eat local (which means seasonal too), for both economic and environmental reasons – local food uses fewer food miles to reach your table. And make the most of fresh, frozen, canned and dried fruit and veg. There are so many good frozen vegetable and fruit mixes available now both from supermarkets and farm shops that I keep a good selection ready in the freezer. But try not to buy too many ready-prepared fresh vegetable packs: they are incredibly expensive and vegetables start to lose their nutrients once cut, so you aren't getting the best from your ingredients. I only use them in emergencies or if really short of time.

Aim to serve a mix of both cooked and raw veg and fruit, and avoid too many smoothies and juices – my dentist hates them as there is now evidence that the fruit acids they contain can have a serious effect on tooth enamel. Just serve them as an occasional treat with a meal and drink plain water during the rest of the day.

Pulses

Beans, lentils and peas (also peanuts, which come from the same family and are not a nut at all!) are the veggie cook's secret weapon. And no, I don't mean because of the effect they can have on the digestion! They are fantastic cheap sources of protein and valuable minerals such as iron, calcium and zinc. And these days they come in so many incarnations, all of which make life easy for the cook – the days of soaking and lengthy cooking can be relegated to the past, although you could invest in one of the new generation of pressure cookers that really take the time out of cooking dried pulses. As ever, the more convenient the more expensive, so if you're on a budget try to plan ahead. Your own soaked and cooked dried chickpeas and beans will have the best

texture and flavour, but I do admit I tend to rely mainly on cans for the best balance of speed and convenience. Pouches of ready-cooked lentils are a luxury I'm keen to avoid unless under pressure.

Grains

Back in the 1970s when I studied at Leith's School of Food and Wine, wholefoods had a rather dismal reputation. Cranks restaurant chain had launched, and while they sold wonderful bowls of salads, the overall impression of their menu was very brown and worthy – and a lot of that was down to the brown wholegrains. Vegetarian food has been trying to throw off that worthy reputation ever since – a real pity for a way of eating based on the most colourful section of the food spectrum. So I am not advocating mountains of brown rice and pasta as the base for your menus – unless you really love them. But rice, pasta, bread and cereals such as porridge and muesli do play an important role in the diet and, with pulses, should make up another third of your plate. I'm really not a fan of wholemeal pasta as it seems to overwhelm sauces but I do love wholegrain rice and bread so serve them with my soups, curries and veg stews.

We are so lucky these days when it comes to the wide selection available; we really are spoilt for choice. If you can, buy the best-quality rice and pasta and you should really notice the difference in taste and texture. After all, you are saving by not buying expensive meat all the time, so I recommend you splash out on good-quality basics.

Nuts and seeds

Rich in essential oils and minerals and vitamins, they really are super foods for the veggie cook, as they also add flavour, texture and interest to so many dishes. Back when I learnt to cook we really didn't use seeds much at all, and the only nuts were the walnuts, hazelnuts and almonds we used in baking. But now there are really good mixes available, all perfect for adding to bread, biscuits and cakes,

scattering over breakfast muesli, topping vegetable gratins, or salads and stir fries. Remember that, because nuts and seeds contain natural oils, you need to use them up or they will go rancid. I tend to have a mad muesli- or flapjack-making session (see the recipe on page 202) after an inspection of my store cupboard shows lots of little packets heading towards their use-by date. I also go through regular patches of sprouting my own seeds, particularly in the vegetable 'famine' months of March and April when nothing is growing in the garden. Sprouted seeds have the highest levels of vitamins and minerals of all foods, and they are fun to grow on the windowsill. There is something wonderfully Blue Peter about the whole process.

Dairy – cheese and eggs

One of the big risks for new veggies is that they replace meat with lots of dairy produce, which is high in saturated fat, particularly in the early stages of transferring to a mainly veggie diet. We can easily overdose on too much high-fat cheese and its natural partner, pasta. Going completely veggie overnight is likely to play havoc with your digestive system: if you and/or your family are considering giving up or reducing your meat intake, then I recommend that you do it in stages, or your gut will tell you in no uncertain terms how it feels about the rapid unexpected change in diet!

Aim to eat a variety of pulses, beans, nuts, seeds and soya products as suggested above, and add free-range eggs as a valuable source of calcium, protein and vitamins. Luckily advice on cholesterol and eggs has now changed and it seems we can happily eat them without raising levels – good news for me as my happy hens keep on laying and I do love their eggs. Milk, cheese and yogurt are all valuable parts of a vegetarian diet, but do watch fat levels and choose low-fat varieties where appropriate. As I have said elsewhere, when cooking for strict vegetarians, avoid cheeses made with rennet. Vegans eat no animal products at all so if

cooking for them you will need to go for non-dairy soya, almond or rice 'milk' and soya 'cheeses'.

Instead of snacking on cheese and biscuits, my suggestion for quick easy eating is a fridge full of what I call grazing foods – they range from slices of tortilla, hummus, maybe a lentil salad, or leftover chickpea curry. If I am really short on time, I might get in some good-quality shop-bought versions but read the labels carefully. Then all you need to do is make up a large salad, defrost some bread and/or homemade soup, and you have the basis of a good meal, either for yourself, or a posse of ravenous teenagers.

On the subject of appetite, where a recipe says it serves four, that's based on the average family of two adults and two medium-sized children. If you are feeding hungry teenage boys or active girls, then the recipes will probably do for two or three.

For more detailed advice on what to keep in your store cupboard, fridge and freezer I do recommend *The Busy Mum's Cookbook*, the precursor to this book. More than half the recipes, if not more, are veggie-friendly and there is lots of useful advice on ingredients, shopping and storing that I won't repeat here.

General tips for children and meal times

As mums, we do need to go with the flow and choose which battles to engage in. You can't force a child to eat when he or she really doesn't want to. My children all went through their picky moments, and at times I felt sure they would end up as bad-mannered table hooligans (they didn't). My advice is to serve good, well-made healthy food but allow for some degree of personal taste.

When it comes to encouraging children to eat what they originally turned their noses up at, don't give up – the trick is to keep calm and go on encouraging everyone to try everything. Even if you've got a child playing power games, take a deep breath and show an air of unconcern while serving them up what everyone else is having. Tastes do

Cooking tips

- All spoonfuls are level
- Imperial v. metric – stick with one set of measurements and don't jump between
- Dishes and tins – use the size specified or the timings will be different. I've tried to keep to a small range of tins and baking dishes as they are the ones I use at home
- Raw or lightly cooked egg dishes should not be served to the very young, infirm or elderly

change and as a parent of now-omnivorous young adults, I speak from experience when I say persevere. It was a special moment when other parents commented on what good manners my children had and I realised my efforts were having an effect. It turned out the little monsters at home, who had to be repeatedly reminded of the basics, turned into little angels (well, on the way to) when eating out. Something must have been working. Good habits take a lot of establishing but, once you get there they stick.

One last thing…

Oh, and by the way, I'd like to apologise to all the busy dads, singletons and students who have been supportive fans of my first Busy Mum's book and will undoubtedly use this one too. I know you are just as worthy of a book dedicated to you and that this should really be the busy everybody's vegetarian cookbook but I'm a mum and have written this from a mum's viewpoint. But I know you are all out there enjoying my books, so thanks for getting in touch, and I'll ask the publisher to do a version just for you.

family favourites

Every mum has a set of dishes hard-wired into her brain that she returns to again and again. The shopping list, preparation and cooking are all on auto-pilot; we know just how much to cook, how long it takes and who will eat what. Here is my collection of those family favourites – after a heated discussion around my kitchen table about the best recipes to include. There are no great surprises here, just the bedrock for a cook's veggie repertoire. Their very familiarity means they also make the perfect introduction for sceptics: anyone who likes lasagne, shepherd's pie and chilli con carne will like these dishes. I'm confident they stand alone as great food – vegetarian or otherwise. ⟶

Roasted root veg with horseradish sauce and baby onion Yorkshires

Like many people I sometimes think the best thing about a roast lunch is all the trimmings. While some vegetarians complain that's all they get at some houses, this recipe makes the point that sometimes it's the meat that's the added extra. Make the batter ahead and leave to stand for 30 minutes and it will improve the finish.

→ Serve with the onion gravy on page 196.

Serves 4
Prepare 15 minutes
Cook 55 minutes

1 medium swede
2 parsnips
2 medium carrots
1 large sweet potato
4 tbsp olive oil
2 sprigs fresh thyme
50g (2oz) plain flour
1 small egg
100ml (4fl oz) semi-skimmed milk
1 small red onion, thinly sliced
4 tbsp soured cream
1 tbsp horseradish sauce
2 tbsp snipped chives
salt and freshly ground black pepper

1 Preheat the oven to 220°C/fan oven 200°C/Gas Mark 7. Peel all the root vegetables and cut them into large even-sized chunks. Place all except the sweet potato in a pan of cold water to cover, bring to the boil and simmer for 5 minutes then drain. Place 3 tablespoons of the oil in a large roasting tin and heat in the oven until smoking. Add all the vegetables including the sweet potato, and baste with the hot oil. Season and snip the thyme sprigs over the tin. Roast for 25 minutes then turn the vegetables and return to the oven for a further 20–25 minutes until crisp and golden.

2 While the vegetables are cooking, sift the flour and seasoning into a bowl. Whisk in the egg and milk to give a smooth batter. Divide the remaining oil between 12 mini muffin tins then add the sliced red onion, and heat in the oven for 5 minutes until the onion is golden. Pour in the batter and return to the oven for 12–15 minutes alongside the vegetables, until the Yorkshires are puffy and golden.

3 Mix together the soured cream, horseradish and chives. Spoon into a serving dish and serve with the roasted vegetables, mini Yorkshires and a jug of onion gravy.

Roasted red onion, goat's cheese and spinach lasagne

This gets my family's vote as one of the best lasagnes ever, and mine for the easy preparation. Use frozen chopped spinach for real speed and convenience – it also has a great flavour and colour. If you've steered clear of frozen spinach after unpleasant memories as a child, you're in for a nice surprise. Today's version is vibrant and tasty.

→ Serve with a green salad.

Serves 6
Prepare 25 minutes
Cook 1 hour 15 minutes

4 large tomatoes, halved
3 medium red onions, cut into wedges
1 tsp dried oregano
1 tbsp olive oil
1 tbsp sun-dried tomato paste
350g (12oz) frozen chopped spinach
50g (2oz) butter
50g (2oz) plain flour
750ml (1¼ pints) semi-skimmed milk
200g (7oz) fresh lasagne sheets
150g (5oz) rinded soft goat's cheese, thinly sliced
4 tbsp grated Parmesan
salt and freshly ground black pepper

1 Preheat the oven to 200°C/fan oven 180°C/Gas Mark 6. Place the tomatoes and onions in a roasting tin in a single layer and scatter over the oregano, oil and seasoning. Roast for 30–35 minutes until tender and just charred. Stir in the tomato paste. Cook the spinach according to pack instructions, drain thoroughly and season.

2 Make the white sauce. Melt the butter in a non-stick pan and stir in the flour. Cook for a minute, stirring, then off the heat, beat in the milk a little at a time – keeping the mixture smooth. Return to the heat and stir until the sauce boils and thickens to the consistency of single cream. Simmer for 2–3 minutes then season.

3 Spread a little of the white sauce over the base of a buttered 2 litre (3½ pint) shallow baking dish. Arrange a layer of pasta over the top, then a layer of the roasted vegetables, followed by the spinach, then the goat's cheese, then sauce. Continue layering up sauce, pasta, vegetables and cheese. Finish with a layer of pasta topped with a thin layer of white sauce. Scatter with grated Parmesan.

4 Bake for 40–45 minutes until bubbling and golden, and the pasta is tender. Cover the top loosely with foil if it gets too brown.

Busy mum's lifesaver Use fresh pasta here rather than dried, as this recipe has less sauce than a classic meat lasagne – the dried variety will not cook as well, and could end up hard and dry. If you have to use dried lasagne, pre-cook the sheets in boiling water until tender, according to pack instructions, before adding.

It's worth knowing that a tablespoon of sun-dried tomato paste really lifts a lot of dishes and is not as acidic as plain tomato purée. Use it as you would Worcestershire sauce (which can't be used in vegetarian cookery as it contains fish).

Mexican-style halloumi fajitas with sweetcorn salsa

Self-assembly fajitas are a real winner – everyone can get involved in the preparation to ensure their own favourite ingredient is included. Lay out all the elements on the table, keep the tortillas warm and let everyone assemble their own.

→ Serve with diced avocado and shredded iceberg lettuce.

Serves 3–4
Prepare 10 minutes
Cook 30 minutes

1 tsp ground cumin
½ tsp chilli powder
¼ tsp ground cinnamon
250g (9oz) pack halloumi cheese, cut into strips
2 red and yellow peppers, deseeded and sliced
2 tsp olive oil
200g can sweetcorn, drained
6 spring onions, sliced
½ red chilli, deseeded and chopped
3 tbsp chopped fresh coriander
juice of 1 lime
1 tbsp dark muscovado sugar
6–8 tortillas
salt and freshly ground black pepper

1 Preheat the oven to 200°C/fan oven 180°C/Gas Mark 6. Mix together the spices and seasoning and rub over the halloumi. Toss the sliced peppers in the oil and arrange over the base of a roasting tin. Roast for 20–25 minutes until charred and tender, adding the halloumi for the final 5 minutes.

2 While the peppers are cooking make the salsa. Mix together the sweetcorn, spring onions, red chilli, coriander and seasoning. Stir in the lime juice and sugar. Heat a non-stick frying pan over a medium heat. Add the tortillas and cook for a minute on each side.

3 To serve, let everyone assemble their own wraps.

Busy mum's lifesaver The spice mix works just as well with chicken. Use 300g (10oz) chicken mini fillets or sliced chicken breast and cook for 25–30 minutes when you roast the peppers. For a non-dairy veggie version substitute smoked tofu.

Look out for corn tortillas for anyone who wants to cut down on wheat in their diet – they have a great flavour and texture.

Spicy vegetable cottage pie with sweet potato mash

Comfort food for all the family but without the meat. The shepherd in his cottage may take issue with this recipe, but I would argue that the spice balances the sweetness of the potato mix, and the lentils have enough texture to satisfy the palate.

→ Serve with frozen peas or broccoli.

Serves 4–6
Prepare 20 minutes
Cook 1 hour

1 tbsp olive oil
1 small onion, finely chopped
1 medium carrot, diced
2 medium leeks, thinly sliced
200g (7oz) green lentils
1 tbsp smoked paprika
2 tbsp tomato ketchup
4–5 tbsp chopped flat-leaf parsley
500ml (17fl oz) vegetable stock
750g (1¾lb) old potatoes, peeled and cubed
350g (12oz) sweet potatoes, peeled and cubed
25g (1oz) butter
salt and freshly ground black pepper

1 Preheat the oven to 200°C/fan oven 180°C/Gas Mark 6. Heat the oil in a large non-stick frying pan or sauté pan and cook the onion, carrot and leeks for 3–4 minutes until softened. Add the lentils then stir in the paprika, ketchup and parsley. Add the stock and seasoning and bring to the boil. Simmer half covered for 25–30 minutes, stirring occasionally, until thickened. Transfer to a 2 litre (3½ pint) shallow ovenproof dish.

2 While the vegetables and lentils are cooking, place the two types of potatoes in separate pans with just enough cold water to cover. Bring to the boil and simmer for 10–15 minutes until tender. Drain the potatoes thoroughly, return to their pans and mash with the butter and seasoning until smooth. Stir both mashes together but don't overmix – you want to create a marbled effect.

3 Spoon the potato over the top of the lentil mixture to cover completely. Rough up the surface with a fork. Bake for 25–30 minutes until golden.

Busy mum's lifesaver Make double quantities and use half for individual pies in foil containers with lids (you can buy them in the supermarket), then freeze for emergencies. Cook from frozen at 190°C/fan oven 170°C/Gas Mark 5 for 45–50 minutes until piping hot all the way through. For vegans omit the butter in the mash and replace with two tablespoons of good olive oil.

Spicy bean and potato chilli

This chilli will convince even the most rampant carnivore that vegetarian food tastes better than they expected. I've cooked it many times for meat-eating friends, many of whom have decided they'll cook this version in future. And it's a hit at student parties.

→ Serve with a green salad and, if you don't want to use the baguette topping, warm up some tortillas instead. Guacamole goes well with this dish.

Serves 4–6
Prepare 15 minutes
Cook 35 minutes

1 tbsp olive oil
1 large onion, finely chopped
1 medium carrot, diced
1 clove garlic, finely chopped
2 tsp each ground cumin and
   smoked paprika
½ –1 tsp chilli powder, depending
   on taste
1 tbsp dried oregano
500g carton tomato passata
1 tbsp sun-dried tomato paste
200ml (7fl oz) vegetable stock
2 x 400g cans red kidney beans,
   drained
350g (12oz) waxy potatoes (such as
   Charlotte), scrubbed and diced
2 char-grilled red peppers from
   a jar, sliced
salt and freshly ground black pepper
sliced baguette and grated Cheddar,
   to finish

1 Heat the oil in a flameproof casserole. Add the onion, carrot and garlic and cook over a medium heat for 3 minutes until softened. Add the cumin, paprika, chilli powder and oregano and cook for a further minute. Stir in the tomato passata, tomato paste, stock and seasoning to taste, and simmer gently for 10 minutes, stirring occasionally.

2 Add the beans, potatoes and peppers to the sauce. Bring to the boil and simmer for a further 12–15 minutes, until the sauce has thickened and the potatoes are tender.

3 Preheat the grill. Arrange the baguette slices on top of the chilli and scatter with the cheese. Grill until bubbling and golden.

Busy mum's lifesaver This dish improves in flavour if made a day or two ahead. Reheat before serving, then add the bread and cheese topping. Try substituting sweet potato for the potato for a change.

   Cheddar is one of the few cheeses that comes in an easily identifiable vegetarian version, made without rennet. Look out, too, for vegetarian goat's cheese and English vegetarian Parmesan.

Creamy leek and potato gratin

This ultra-comforting dish takes its inspiration from the Swedish classic, Jansson's Temptation. The original contains anchovies but I've used leeks and bay leaves for a more fragrant finish.
➡ Serve with steamed broccoli.

Serves 4
Prepare 20 minutes
Cook 1 hour

1 tbsp olive oil
25g (1oz) butter
3 leeks, thinly sliced
2 cloves garlic, finely chopped
1.2kg (2½lb) old potatoes
300ml (½ pint) double cream
300ml (½ pint) full-cream milk
freshly grated nutmeg
2–3 fresh bay leaves, torn in half
salt and freshly ground black pepper

1 Preheat the oven to 190°C/fan oven 170°C/Gas Mark 5. Heat the oil and half the butter in a medium frying pan and add the leeks and garlic. Cook gently for 5 minutes until softened but not coloured. Remove from the heat.

2 Peel the potatoes and cut into thin slices, then cut across the slices into matchsticks. Combine with the leeks and plenty of seasoning and tip into a buttered 1.75 litre (3 pint) shallow ovenproof dish or roasting tin. Level the surface.

3 Whisk together the cream, milk, nutmeg and seasoning and pour over the vegetables. Tuck the bay leaves in amongst the vegetables. Dot with the remaining butter and bake for 50–60 minutes until the potato is tender and the top is golden brown. Cover loosely with foil if the top gets too brown.

Busy mum's lifesaver For fish eaters replace the bay leaves with 6–8 chopped anchovies. Meat eaters can try it with cooked cubes of pancetta. You can also vary the root veg – try a combination of parsnip, swede and celeriac, depending on what you have to hand.

Pimiento, pine nut and pea frittata

Along with risotto, omelettes are one of the most reliable emergency dishes. I always have eggs in the fridge and potatoes and onions in the veg drawer for the basic recipe, and then add whatever other flavourings are available. This Italian frittata is a thick omelette cake made using frozen peas, pine nuts and a jar of pimientos for speed and convenience. Cut the frittata into wedges, and serve warm or at room temperature. If there are any leftovers wrap them up for packed lunches or cut them into cubes to hand round with drinks.

→ Serve with a big green salad.

Serves 4
Prepare 15 minutes
Cook 15 minutes

2 tbsp olive oil
1 large red onion, thinly sliced
150g (5oz) frozen peas
1 pimiento from a jar, sliced
25g (1oz) pine nuts, toasted
6 large free-range eggs
salt and freshly ground black pepper

1 Heat half the oil in a large frying pan and add the onion and plenty of seasoning. Cook over a medium heat for 5 minutes until tender. Blanch the peas in a pan of boiling water for 2 minutes then drain really well. Add to the onions with the pimiento and cook for a couple of minutes. Stir in the pine nuts.

2 Preheat the grill. Break the eggs in a bowl with the seasoning and beat with a fork. Add the hot vegetables from the pan and mix thoroughly. Leave to stand for 5 minutes. Heat the remaining oil in a 20cm (8in) non-stick frying pan until very hot and pour in the egg mixture. Stir with a fork, lifting the middle of the frittata to let the runny egg trickle down into the base. Cook over a medium heat for 3–4 minutes until set and the base is golden.

3 Place the pan under the grill for 2–3 minutes to brown the top. The egg should be set but not dry. Turn out on to a plate and serve.

Busy mum's lifesaver You can buy ready-toasted pine nuts but they are expensive. To do your own, simply dry-fry them in a small frying pan over a medium heat for a minute or two until pale golden. Take care not to burn them or they will taste bitter. Vary the flavourings according to the season: try broad bean and feta or asparagus and goat's cheese. Just fry the onion as instructed and add to the eggs with the lightly cooked veg and diced cheese. Add cubed pancetta for meat eaters.

Spinach, tomato and chickpea curry

Really quick, easy and versatile – this is one of my five-star recipes: I make no apology for including it again here, as well as in my first Busy Mum's book. Vary the veg according to season and what's to hand: add peas or green beans instead of spinach or even quickly fried aubergine slices.

→ Serve with the cucumber and walnut raita on page 196 and warm naan bread for the easiest curry.

Serves 4
Prepare 15 minutes
Cook 25 minutes

1 tbsp sunflower oil
1 clove garlic, chopped
1 small onion, finely chopped
small piece fresh root ginger, peeled and chopped
1 tbsp medium curry paste
400g can chopped tomatoes
400g can chickpeas, including canning liquid
250g (9oz) fresh spinach, roughly shredded
salt and freshly ground black pepper

1 Heat the oil in a medium saucepan and cook the garlic, onion and ginger together for 5 minutes until softened and golden. Stir in the curry paste and cook for a minute then add the tomatoes and simmer for 5 minutes to make a thick sauce, stirring occasionally.

2 Stir in the chickpeas with their liquid and bring to the boil. Simmer for 10 minutes then season and stir in the spinach. Cook gently together for a couple of minutes until the spinach is just cooked. Check seasoning and serve with the raita.

Busy mum's lifesaver I often make double quantities of the base tomato sauce then freeze half. Just thaw when needed and continue as above. Buy frozen leaf spinach and frozen chopped ginger and you'll always have the ingredients to hand. If you haven't got chickpeas in the cupboard, use any kind of canned beans; I've even used cubed new potatoes as an alternative, cooking them in the sauce for slightly longer. For the meat-eating contingent of the family this dish goes really well with chicken tikka.

Celebrate summer vegetable stew

This stew makes the most of the lovely veg that all seem to arrive at once in summer. Small children love anything with peas and baby carrots in, so it's a good way of introducing them to yet more veg. I got into the habit of stirring pesto into all kinds of dishes, as my children love it – and it's ideal here. ⟶ Served with lots of bread, it's sustaining enough for a main course.

Serves 4
Prepare 10 minutes
Cook 25 minutes

2 tbsp olive oil
1 small onion, finely chopped
1 stick celery, chopped
100g (4oz) baby carrots, trimmed
2 cloves garlic, finely chopped
250g (9oz) new potatoes, quartered
600ml (1 pint) vegetable stock
500g (1lb 2oz) each peas and broad
    beans, podded (or 100g/4oz each
    ready-podded)
100g (4oz) green beans, trimmed
    and halved
3 tbsp chopped fresh mint
4 tbsp basil pesto
4 tbsp double cream
salt and freshly ground black pepper

1 Heat the oil in a large pan and add the onion, celery, carrots and garlic. Cook gently, stirring, for 5 minutes, then add the potatoes and cook for another 5 minutes. Add the stock and seasoning and simmer for 10–15 minutes until the potatoes are tender.

2 Add the peas, broad beans and green beans and simmer for a further 5 minutes until the vegetables are just tender. Remove from the heat and add the mint.

3 To serve, spoon into warm bowls. Mix together the pesto and cream and drizzle over the stew.

Busy mum's lifesaver For a non-dairy pesto, simply whiz up a handful of basil with toasted pine nuts, crushed garlic, a little grated lemon rind and a spoonful or two of extra-virgin olive oil. Stir into the stew, leaving out the cream. Add more stock to turn the stew into a soup or whiz up any leftovers for a smooth soup and serve it chilled.

Spicy rice

An easy version of paella and a great way to get small children to eat more unusual vegetables such as courgettes, which they might turn down if served in a more recognisable form. It worked with mine! Although we've always referred to this recipe as spicy rice at home, it isn't really very spicy at all.

Serves 4
Prepare 15 minutes
Cook 30 minutes

2 tbsp olive oil
1 small onion, finely chopped
2 cloves garlic, finely chopped
1 medium courgette, diced
100g (4oz) green beans, halved
1 medium aubergine, cubed
2 canned pimientos, drained
  and sliced
2 tomatoes, diced
1 tbsp smoked paprika
230g (8oz) risotto or paella rice
750ml (1¼ pints) simmering
  vegetable stock
salt and freshly ground black pepper

1 Preheat the oven to 190°C/fan oven 170°C/Gas Mark 5. Heat the oil in a medium-size shallow flameproof casserole or gratin dish over a medium heat. Add the onion and garlic and cook for 3 minutes, stirring occasionally, until softened but not browned. Stir in the courgette, beans, aubergine and pimientos, turn up the heat and continue cooking for a further 5 minutes, stirring occasionally, until the vegetables are lightly browned.

2 Stir in the tomatoes, paprika and rice and continue cooking for 1 minute. Add the stock and seasoning, turn up the heat and bring to the boil, stirring occasionally.

3 Transfer to the oven for 15–20 minutes until the rice is just tender and lightly browned on top. Loosely cover the pan with foil and leave to stand for about 5 minutes, then fork up the rice and serve.

Busy mum's lifesaver This rice dish can be made more substantial by adding a can of drained chickpeas at step 2. For meat eaters it goes really well with grilled sausages or other pork dishes.

Green summer risotto

Risottos are my (and my family's) idea of the perfect comfort food. They're so convenient – you've always got the makings of one in the cupboard or veg drawer. You can make risottos in all the colours of the rainbow: just follow this basic method and vary the vegetables. Pumpkin, aubergine and courgette are all great; this version makes the most of my abundant herb garden.

Serves 4–6
Prepare 15 minutes
Cook 25 minutes

450g (1lb) prepared seasonal
   vegetables (such as small
   courgettes, podded peas,
   green beans, broad beans
   and asparagus tips)
2 tbsp olive oil
2 shallots, finely chopped
1–2 cloves garlic, finely chopped
350g (12oz) arborio risotto rice
about 1.5 litres (2½ pints) simmering
   vegetable stock, made with a cube
100ml (4fl oz) dry white wine
50g (2oz) butter
50g (2oz) fresh mixed herbs, such as
   flat-leaf parsley, basil, chives,
   tarragon, dill or chervil, finely
   chopped
50g (2oz) freshly grated Parmesan
salt and freshly ground black pepper

1 Cook the vegetables in simmering water for 2–3 minutes until almost tender. Drain and plunge into iced water to cool. Drain thoroughly and set aside. Heat the oil in a heavy-based saucepan. Add the shallots and garlic and cook for about 3 minutes until softened. Add the rice and stir to coat in the oil.

2 Add a ladleful of stock and the white wine to the pan and simmer over a medium-low heat until the liquid is absorbed, stirring. Continue adding the stock, a ladleful at a time, stirring until it has been absorbed, before adding the next lot. Carry on until all the stock is absorbed and the rice is tender and creamy but still with a slight bite. This should take about 20 minutes.

3 While the rice is cooking, place the butter in a blender or food processor with the herbs and seasoning and process until well blended together. When the rice is tender, add the reserved vegetables and cook for another minute or two to heat through. Stir in the herb butter and Parmesan and adjust the seasoning. Serve immediately.

Busy mum's lifesaver To get ahead, use the chef's method for risotto and cook it up to the first stage – adding the rice and first amount of liquid. Then just remove from the heat and set aside. When you are ready to cook the risotto, reheat the rice and carry on. Serve with grilled lamb, chicken or fish for meat eaters.

Easy cannellini bean, egg and red onion salad

This bean salad is so quick to prepare, it's a regular in our household – especially for a summer lunch outside. It's worth buying the best-quality canned beans for this dish when you want to spoil yourself, as the texture and flavour make a noticeable difference. For an everyday lunch I tend to use the economy range. For smaller children I think lots of dressing is important, so the food is not dry. (This was one of those dishes that converted my children to salad so I'm speaking from experience!)
→ Serve with plenty of bread to mop up the dressing.

Serves 2–3
Prepare 15 minutes
Cook 25 minutes

1 red pepper
2 free-range eggs
400g can cannellini beans, drained
1 medium red onion, finely sliced
4–6 ripe tomatoes, cut into quarters
6–8 black olives, stoned
1 tbsp balsamic vinegar
3–4 tbsp extra-virgin olive oil
3 tbsp chopped flat-leaf parsley
    and basil
salt and freshly ground black pepper

1 Preheat the grill to high. Place the pepper on the grill pan and grill for about 5 minutes, turning occasionally, until blackened. Place in a plastic bag for 2 minutes for the skin to loosen. When cool enough to handle, remove the skin, deseed and cut into strips. Place the eggs in a pan of cold water and bring to the boil. Simmer for 8 minutes, drain and run under cold water. Shell and cut into wedges.

2 Place the beans, onion, tomatoes and olives in a shallow serving bowl. Whisk together the vinegar, oil, herbs and seasoning and pour over the salad. Toss to coat in the dressing. Arrange the egg wedges and pepper strips on top.

Busy mum's lifesaver Substitute ready-cooked pimientos from a jar for convenience but do have a go at grilling your own peppers if possible, as the flavour is wonderful. This is a salad where all the flavours are better if not too chilled. Try adding cooked French beans, rocket or watercress and, for fish eaters, drained tuna.

food in
a hurry

When time is tight and tummies are rumbling, turn to pasta and rice for convenience and security. They're always there in the store cupboard, won't break the bank, and there are so many wonderful ways to cook and serve them. What's more, it's so easy to adjust quantities, depending on who arrives in the kitchen and how hungry everyone is. My main piece of advice is to buy good-quality basics: there is a huge difference in taste and texture, so much so that even children will notice. My daughter gets very sniffy about cheap pasta, and rages at her house-mates when they use up all her durum wheat pasta. →

Penne with mushrooms and garlic breadcrumbs

If your household's anything like mine, there's always leftover bread. Instead of adding more breadcrumbs to the freezer, this is a great Italian method for using up stale bread that adds wonderful texture and crunch to pasta. It's so simple but totally delicious. Mushroom lovers will enjoy it as their flavour really sings out when treated in this way.

Serves 4
Prepare 5 minutes
Cook 15 minutes

2 cloves garlic, chopped
1 tsp capers
4 tbsp chopped flat-leaf parsley
1 stale ciabatta roll, cut into chunks
3 tbsp olive oil
350g (12oz) good-quality penne pasta
250g (9oz) white mushrooms, sliced
salt and freshly ground black pepper

1 Place the garlic, capers, parsley, ciabatta and seasoning in a processor or blender and whiz until the mixture forms fine breadcrumbs. Heat a tablespoon of the oil in a small non-stick frying pan and cook the breadcrumb mixture for a couple of minutes until crisp and golden. Remove from the pan and set aside.

2 Bring a large pan of water to the boil and cook the penne for 10–12 minutes until tender or according to pack instructions. While the pasta is cooking, heat the remaining oil in the frying pan and add the mushrooms. Cook over a high heat for 3–4 minutes until golden, then stir in the breadcrumbs. Cook for a minute. Drain the pasta and toss with the mushrooms. Serve immediately.

Busy mum's lifesaver Use readymade white breadcrumbs if you don't have any stale ciabatta. Make up double the crumb mixture and you can sprinkle it on grilled vegetables, such as courgettes or peppers, with a dash or two of good olive oil for a really simple lunch.

Broccoli and sunflower seed pasta with lemon oregano dressing

Funnily enough my family have always loved broccoli and I often make double of this dish and keep half back for packed lunches and picnics – it's delicious hot or cold. Fresh oregano pairs really well with lemon but don't be tempted to use dried, as it's too strong – substitute chopped parsley instead.

➡ Serve with the sun-dried soda bread on page 188.

Serves 4
Prepare 10 minutes
Cook 10 minutes

300g (10oz) pasta shells or twists
250g (9oz) broccoli, cut into florets
grated rind and juice of 1 unwaxed
    lemon
3 tbsp extra-virgin olive oil
3 tbsp chopped fresh oregano or
    fresh parsley
25g (1oz) sunflower seeds
1 small red onion, sliced
8–10 stoned Kalamata olives, halved
100g (4oz) feta cheese, cubed
    (optional)
salt and freshly ground black pepper

1 Cook the pasta in plenty of boiling water for 10 minutes or according to pack instructions, until tender. Meanwhile cook the broccoli in a pan of boiling water for 3–4 minutes until just tender. Whisk together the lemon rind and juice, olive oil, oregano and seasoning.

2 Drain the pasta and broccoli and toss with the dressing. Add the sunflower seeds, onion, olives and feta if using and mix together. Check the seasoning and serve hot or cold.

Busy mum's lifesaver This is a good way of using up leftover pasta if you've cooked too much for another dish. Keep a jar of the dressing made up in the fridge (it will last for 2–3 days) and toss the extra pasta with some while it's warm. It's easier to coat pasta when it's warm. Cool, cover and leave in the fridge ready for the rest of the ingredients. The recipe also works well with red pepper pesto instead of the lemon dressing.

Creamy Roquefort, spinach and walnut pasta

The flavours in this richly flavoured pasta dish may seem quite adult, but many children like them too. You can use any creamy blue cheese for the sauce – for example, Stilton or a Shropshire blue – but for a real grownups-only treat, try Roquefort. It's the most expensive, but a little of it goes a long way and its distinctive salty tang makes all the difference in this recipe.

Serves 4
Prepare 10 minutes
Cook 15 minutes

350g (12oz) pasta shells
150ml (¼ pint) medium white wine
2 cloves garlic, lightly crushed
150g (5oz) Roquefort cheese, diced
4 tbsp crème fraîche
50g (2oz) walnut pieces, roughly
   chopped
300g (10oz) baby spinach, washed
salt and freshly ground black pepper

1 Cook the pasta in boiling water for 10–12 minutes until tender or according to pack instructions. Drain and return to the pan.

2 While the pasta is cooking put the wine and garlic together in a small pan and heat until boiling. Stir in the Roquefort and crème fraîche and simmer for a minute. Spoon out the garlic and stir in the walnuts and spinach. Heat through gently but don't boil. Season to taste and pour over the pasta. Toss to coat and serve.

Busy mum's lifesaver Keep a selection of dried pasta in your store cupboard. To get the best shape for the sauce, use this guide: the thinner and runnier the sauce the longer the pasta needs to be; use short, stubby shapes for thicker, chunkier sauces.

As the wine in the sauce is boiled, the alcohol is all cooked off so it's safe to serve this dish to children.

Tahini-glazed vegetable and noodle stir-fry

Tahini is a paste made from ground sesame seeds, used to add flavour to hummus, which is how I sold it to my children. It's got a lovely peanut-buttery flavour. Here it makes a great sauce that can be used with any combination of vegetables – I like the colour and texture of spring greens and mini carrots together but use whatever you have in the fridge.

Serves 4
Prepare 5 minutes
Cook 10 minutes

350g (12oz) rice noodles
2 tbsp tahini paste
1 tbsp soy sauce
1 tbsp red wine vinegar
1 tbsp dark muscovado sugar
1 tbsp sunflower oil
1 clove garlic, finely chopped
2.5cm (1in) piece fresh root ginger, peeled and finely chopped
½–1 red chilli, deseeded and chopped
450g (1lb) spring greens, shredded
100g (4oz) Chantenay carrots, trimmed and halved lengthways
1 tbsp sesame seeds

1 Pour boiling water over the noodles and leave to stand for 5 minutes. Mix the tahini paste, soy sauce, vinegar and sugar together and set aside.

2 Heat the oil in a wok or large frying pan over a high heat until almost smoking. Add the garlic, ginger and chilli and stir-fry for 30 seconds, then add the greens and carrots and continue stir-frying for 3–4 minutes or until just tender.

3 Drain the noodles and add to the pan, along with the tahini mixture, and stir-fry together for 2 minutes until completely heated through. Sprinkle with sesame seeds and serve immediately.

Busy mum's lifesaver Tahini paste comes in two versions, dark and light. The only difference is that, in the dark variety, the seeds have been toasted, which intensifies the nutty flavour. If your jar of tahini has oil floating on top, stir it through the paste before using, as the excess oil will affect the texture. In an emergency, use peanut butter instead. For meat eaters, try adding prawns or pancetta cubes and stir-frying quickly before you add the vegetables.

Squash, green beans and pesto gnocchi bake

This dish is colourful and easy – and a great one for teenagers to cook for themselves. Look for readymade potato gnocchi in the chiller cabinet at the supermarket or on the shelf with the pasta. I suggest you choose a good Italian brand as some gnocchi can be a bit heavy and sticky.

→ Serve the bake with a tomato salad.

Serves 4
Prepare 10 minutes
Cook 40 minutes

I small butternut squash, peeled, deseeded and cubed
200g (7oz) trimmed fine green beans, halved
250g (9oz) new potatoes, halved
500g pack potato gnocchi
150g (5oz) carton good-quality basil pesto
3–4 tbsp freshly grated Parmesan
3 tbsp white breadcrumbs
salt and freshly ground black pepper

1 Preheat the oven to 200°C/fan oven 180°C/Gas Mark 6. Cook the squash in boiling water for 10 minutes until tender, adding the beans for the last 3–4 minutes. Drain.

2 Cook the potatoes in boiling water for 15–20 minutes until tender, then drain. Cook the gnocchi in a pan of boiling water for 2–3 minutes. Drain thoroughly and add to the vegetables. Toss with the pesto until thoroughly coated and season to taste.

3 Tip the gnocchi and vegetables into a buttered 1.75 litre (3 pint) shallow ovenproof dish. Top with the Parmesan and breadcrumbs and bake for 15–20 minutes until golden.

Busy mum's lifesaver Use a 350g (12oz) pack of ready-prepared butternut squash for convenience. Look for the V symbol on the label when buying readymade pesto for strict vegetarians: it means it's been made with vegetarian cheese.

Pasta with roasted aubergine, red onions and goat's cheese

The secret to this dish is to roast the aubergines until they are really tender and well browned to bring out their true sweet smoky flavour. This is one of Henry, my stepson's favourite pasta dishes. He's my regular tester when I'm working and after trying this, aubergines are now one of his favourite vegetables. This dish also makes a lovely salad served at room temperature.

➡ Serve with a big leafy salad.

Serves 4
Prepare 10 minutes
Cook 30 minutes

2 medium aubergines, trimmed and
    cut into wedges
2 medium red onions, cut into wedges
3–4 cloves garlic, finely chopped
4 tbsp extra-virgin olive oil
large handful fresh basil, shredded
300g (10oz) penne pasta
200g (7oz) soft goat's cheese
25g (1oz) toasted pine nuts
salt and freshly ground black pepper
a few extra basil leaves and freshly
    grated Parmesan, to serve

1 Preheat the oven to 220°C/fan oven 200°C/Gas Mark 7. Arrange the aubergine and onion wedges in a roasting tin in a single layer and scatter over the garlic, oil, basil and seasoning. Roast for 25–30 minutes, turning the vegetables halfway through cooking, until well browned and tender.

2 Meanwhile, cook the pasta in a large pan of boiling water for 10–12 minutes or according to pack instructions, until just tender. Drain well and return to the pan. Add the roasted vegetables, goat's cheese, pine nuts and seasoning and toss together until well mixed. Serve scattered with a few basil leaves and Parmesan.

Busy mum's lifesaver This makes a good bake if you want to prepare ahead. Spoon the cooked pasta and veg into a buttered shallow ovenproof dish. Then when you're ready to cook, top with grated Parmesan and drizzle with a little olive oil and bake for 10–15 minutes in a preheated medium hot oven (190°C/fan oven 170°C/Gas Mark 5).

Hearty pasta, white bean and rosemary soup

Pasta and bean soups are perfect comfort food – an ideal Saturday lunch in the depths of winter. Any leftovers can be reheated and packed into a flask to take to work or school (but add more water when reheating as the pasta absorbs a lot of the liquid if left to sit). Canned chickpeas are a good alternative to cannellini beans.

➡ Serve with crusty Italian bread such as focaccia.

Serves 4
Prepare 10 minutes
Cook 30 minutes

1 tbsp olive oil
1 large onion, finely chopped
2 sticks celery, sliced
1 small leek, thinly sliced
2 cloves garlic, chopped
2 large sprigs fresh rosemary,
   leaves chopped
400g can chopped Italian tomatoes
400g can cannellini beans, drained
200g (7oz) small soup pasta
salt and freshly ground black pepper
extra-virgin olive oil, to serve
freshly grated Cheddar or Parmesan,
   to serve

1 Heat the oil in a heavy-based pan, add the onion, celery, leek and garlic and cook over a low heat for 5 minutes until softened. Add the rosemary, tomatoes and seasoning, bring to the boil and simmer for 5 minutes to give a thick sauce.

2 Add the beans to the pan and cook for a further 3 minutes then add 1 litre (1¾ pints) water and bring to the boil. Add the pasta, bring back to the boil and simmer vigorously for 10–12 minutes until the pasta is tender. Check seasoning.

3 Spoon into warm serving bowls and serve with extra-virgin olive oil for drizzling and grated Cheddar or Parmesan.

Busy mum's lifesaver Dried beans have a wonderful flavour and texture; they're worth cooking when you have the time. Cover 200g (7oz) beans in cold water and leave them overnight or for at least 8 hours. Drain, add plenty of fresh cold water to cover, plus flavourings such as an onion, carrot, celery stick and bay leaf, and cook for an hour or two, until tender. Use the cooking liquid in the soup. Cook a big batch, toss any leftovers in olive oil, cover and keep in the fridge for up to 3 days to add to salads and stews.

Mushroom and leek pasta bake

A comforting pasta bake – basically a macaroni cheese jazzed up with vegetables – makes a complete all-in-one meal. I've used a strong blue cheese such as Stilton, though you can choose your family's favourite. I always add tomatoes around the edge of the dish as another way of getting more vegetables into the meal.

➡ Serve with frozen peas or broccoli

Serves 4–6
Prepare 15 minutes
Cook 45 minutes

350g (12oz) penne pasta
75g (3oz) butter
2 leeks, thinly sliced
175g (6oz) chestnut mushrooms, sliced
50g (2oz) plain flour
750ml (1¼ pints) semi-skimmed milk
100g (4oz) strong-flavoured blue cheese such as Stilton, grated
1 tsp English mustard
dash of Tabasco sauce
150g (5oz) cherry tomatoes, halved
2 tbsp white breadcrumbs
2 tbsp freshly grated Parmesan
salt and freshly ground black pepper

1 Preheat the oven to 200°C/fan oven 180°C/ Gas Mark 6. Cook the pasta in plenty of boiling water for 8–10 minutes or according to pack instructions, until just tender. While the pasta is cooking melt 25g (1oz) of the butter in a non-stick frying pan and cook the leeks and mushrooms over a medium heat for about 3–4 minutes until tender. Drain the pasta and arrange in a 1.75 litre (3 pint) ovenproof baking dish. Mix in the leeks and mushrooms.

2 To make the sauce melt the remaining butter in a medium non-stick pan and stir in the flour. Cook for a minute, stirring, then take the pan off the heat and gradually whisk in the milk, keeping the mixture smooth. Return the pan to the heat and stir until thickened. Simmer for 2 minutes, stirring, then off the heat stir in the blue cheese, mustard, Tabasco and seasoning. Pour the sauce over the pasta and vegetables. Arrange the halved tomatoes all around the edge of the dish, cut-side up.

3 Mix the breadcrumbs and Parmesan and sprinkle over the dish. Bake for 25–30 minutes until the top is crisp and golden.

Busy mum's lifesaver You can use any pasta shape for this dish but curly ones will take more sauce so if using them, add a bit more milk – about 100ml (4fl oz) – to the sauce to stretch it further. In a real emergency use a good-quality readymade cheese sauce for pasta, then stir in a bit more cheese.

Thai rice with mushrooms and omelette ribbons

This recipe for egg-fried rice starts from scratch, but you can make up a batch even faster if you have leftover rice in the fridge. Shiitake mushrooms have great flavour and texture but you can substitute regular chestnut mushrooms. The eggs are turned into a herby omelette cut into strips and scattered over the rice for a lovely finish.

➡ Serve with stir-fried broccoli.

Serves 3–4
Prepare 10 minutes
Cook 20 minutes

300g (10oz) Thai jasmine rice
2 tbsp soy sauce
2 tbsp sherry or rice wine
2 tbsp sunflower oil
2 spring onions, chopped
1 clove garlic, finely chopped
230g (8oz) shiitake mushrooms, sliced

For the omelette
3 free-range eggs, beaten
2 tbsp chopped fresh coriander
½ red chilli, deseeded and chopped
salt and freshly ground black pepper

1 Place the rice in a pan with 500ml (17fl oz) water and bring to the boil. Simmer uncovered for about 10 minutes until the water has been absorbed, then cover the pan tightly and leave to stand while you prepare the topping.

2 Mix together the soy sauce, sherry or rice wine and 4 tablespoons water and set aside. Make the omelette by beating the eggs with the coriander, chilli and seasoning. Heat a teaspoon of the oil in a small omelette pan and add the egg mixture. Cook for several minutes until browned on the base. Slide the omelette on to a plate and roll it up, then cut into thin ribbons.

3 Heat the remaining oil in a wok or non-stick frying pan and add the spring onions, garlic and mushrooms. Stir-fry for a couple of minutes until lightly browned then add the soy mixture and stir for a further minute or two until the mushrooms are cooked. To serve, transfer the rice to a warmed shallow serving dish then spoon over the mushrooms and top with the omelette strips.

Busy mum's lifesaver Mushrooms are like sponges so absorb water. The trick is to wipe rather than wash them and to cook them quickly over a high heat so they brown and retain some texture. Then children are more likely to enjoy them.

Linguine with grilled pepper and peas

My children love the sweet flavour of grilled peppers and peas. The sauce in this dish is made from French soft cheese with garlic and herbs – a real taste of my childhood and ideal for using in cooking. Pick a brand such as Boursin, which is made without rennet so is suitable for strict vegetarians.
➡ Serve with a mixed leaf salad.

Serves 4
Prepare 15 minutes
Cook 15 minutes

3 red peppers
350g (12oz) linguine pasta
100g (4oz) frozen peas
2 tbsp olive oil
100g (4oz) soft cheese with herbs
    and garlic
2 tbsp single cream
4 tbsp shredded fresh basil
salt and freshly ground black pepper
freshly grated Parmesan, to serve

1 Preheat the grill to high. Place the peppers on the grill pan and grill for about 5 minutes, turning occasionally, until blackened. Place them in a plastic bag for 2 minutes for the skin to loosen. When cool enough to handle, remove the skin, deseed them and cut into strips.

2 Cook the pasta in a large pan of boiling water for 10–12 minutes or according to pack instructions, until just tender. Meanwhile, cook the peas in a pan of boiling water for 2 minutes until just tender and drain.

3 Heat the oil in a large frying pan over a medium heat. Add the pepper and cook for 1 minute, stirring, then add the cheese and cream and cook for a further minute. Add the peas and seasoning. Drain the pasta and add to the pan with the basil. Toss well. Serve with grated Parmesan.

Busy mum's lifesaver For meat eaters, add quickly cooked pancetta or chorizo cubes to this dish – they'll love it.

Roasted pepper risotto

This dish is so full-flavoured that it leaves everyone feeling satisfied – the key is to cook the peppers until they are really charred, to caramelise the sugars and bring out the sweet flavour. Any leftovers make delicious little fried croquettes. For meat lovers it goes perfectly with grilled Italian sausages, especially the ones made with fennel.

➡ Serve with a leafy green salad.

Serves 4
Prepare 15 minutes
Cook 45 minutes

3 large orange, red or yellow peppers
    (a mix is wonderfully colourful)
3 tbsp olive oil
1 small onion, finely chopped
1 clove garlic, chopped
350g (12oz) arborio risotto rice
1 tbsp sun-dried tomato paste
1 litre (1¾ pints) vegetable stock,
    simmering
150ml (¼ pint) dry white wine
100g (4oz) rinded goat's cheese, diced
25g (1oz) butter
salt and freshly ground black pepper

1 Preheat the oven to 200°C/fan oven 180°C/ Gas Mark 6. Place the peppers on a roasting tin and cook for 25–30 minutes until well blackened. Cover with a clean tea towel for 5 minutes to let the skins soften, then skin, deseed and cut into 1cm (¼in) squares.

2 Heat the oil in a medium non-stick pan and cook the onion and garlic together for 3–4 minutes until softened. Stir in the rice and cook for a minute, then stir in the tomato paste. Add a ladleful of stock and the white wine to the pan and simmer over a medium-low heat until the liquid is absorbed, stirring. Continue adding the stock, a ladleful at a time, stirring until it has been absorbed, before adding the next lot. Carry on until all the stock is absorbed and the rice is tender and creamy but still with a slight bite. This should take about 20 minutes.

3 Stir in the goat's cheese, butter and seasoning. Cover and leave to stand for 5 minutes before serving.

Busy mum's lifesaver Use ready-cooked pimientos from a jar to save time, but the flav our won't be quite as good. To make croquettes, roll leftover risotto into walnut-sized balls. Push a basil leaf and a cube of mozzarella into the centre of each, then dip into egg and breadcrumbs and deep fry until golden. Drain on kitchen paper and serve.

party time

Throwing a totally veggie party may seem a challenge too far at first but, with some careful planning and the recipes you'll find here, you'll discover it's a great way to cater for everyone – you may even convert some occasional meat eaters to the delights of meat-free living. And a veggie party is easier on the budget too! This chapter will give you some ideas to get you started. Depending on numbers, I kick off with a couple of interesting canapés, then two or three colourful dishes such as the Italian rice and spinach cake on page 62, served with salads and good bread, then maybe finish off with spectacular but simple puds such as the meringues with rose petals or chocolate raspberry terrine in the puds chapter, and a board of local cheeses. ⟶

Georgia's caponata cups

Spectacular canapés are a great way to start a party. This recipe and the next one have a long list of ingredients but can be prepared well in advance and the results are impressive. Both canapés were created by my daughter's friend Georgia, who is a caterer. To get the best flavour and texture, you need to cook the aubergines in a lot of oil – but as the canapés are tiny, you don't need to worry too much.

Makes 40
Prepare 30 minutes
Cook 40 minutes

3 large aubergines, cut into 1.5cm
    (½in) cubes
4–6 tbsp olive oil
1 large red onion, finely chopped
2 cloves garlic, finely chopped
1 tbsp tarragon vinegar
400g can Italian tomatoes
2 tbsp dark muscovado sugar
1 tbsp chopped fresh oregano
small handful flat-leaf parsley,
    finely chopped
1 tbsp balsamic vinegar
3 tbsp capers, roughly chopped
½ jar stoned green olives,
    roughly chopped
100g (4oz) pine nuts
2 sheets filo pastry
50g (2oz) butter, melted
100g (4oz) dolcelatte or similar soft
    blue cheese (optional)
salt and freshly ground black pepper
chopped chives, to finish

1 Sprinkle the cubed aubergines with a little salt and leave to stand in a colander for 10 minutes. Rinse under running water then pat dry with kitchen paper. Heat 4–5 tablespoons oil in a large frying pan and fry the aubergine in batches till golden. Drain on kitchen paper.

2 Clean the pan, add a tablespoon of oil and cook the onion and garlic over a low heat for 3–4 minutes until softened. Return the aubergine to the pan and add the tarragon vinegar. Stir in the tomatoes and add 1 tablespoon of the sugar. Simmer for 15–20 minutes until the aubergine is cooked through and the sauce thickened. Stir in the remaining sugar, the herbs, balsamic vinegar, capers, olives and seasoning and simmer for a further minute or two. Add the pine nuts right at the end then cool, cover and store in the fridge. The flavours will develop and the pine nuts will soak up the excess oil and add extra texture to the caponata.

3 Preheat the oven to 170°C/fan oven 150°C/Gas Mark 3. Lay a sheet of filo pastry on a chopping board and brush liberally with melted butter then gently lay the second sheet of filo over the top. Brush again, then use a large knife or cutter to cut the sheet into squares roughly 4cm (1½in) square. Push the squares into mini muffin tins and bake for 8–10 minutes until golden. Turn out on to a baking sheet to cool. Store in airtight containers.

4 To assemble, use a teaspoon to fill each case with a little of the caponata mixture then top with a square of dolcelatte if using. Sprinkle chives over the top. Arrange on a plate or tray and serve.

Busy mum's lifesaver This recipe makes double the quantity of caponata that you'll need, so serve the rest on its own as a lovely party salad.

Minted pea and polenta pieces

Make all the elements of these pretty little mouthfuls well in advance – that's the secret to good party planning. Then all you need to do is fry the polenta or cook it in the oven (see note below) and top with the pea purée and pecorino shavings.

Makes 25
Prepare 30 minutes
Cook 20 minutes

For the polenta
175g (6oz) instant polenta
large pinch of dried chillies
25g (1oz) butter
25g (1oz) freshly grated Parmesan
1 large free-range egg, beaten
100g (4oz) dried white breadcrumbs
salt and freshly ground black pepper

For the pea purée topping
200g (7oz) frozen peas
2 cloves garlic, peeled
2 tbsp chopped fresh mint

sunflower oil for deep frying
juice of 1 lemon
mint leaves and pecorino shavings,
   to finish

1 To make the polenta bring 750ml (1¼ pints) water to the boil. Add a generous pinch of salt and the dried chillies, then pour in the polenta, whisking continuously to prevent lumps forming. Lower the heat and simmer for 1–2 minutes until the polenta is thick and leaves the sides of the pan.

2 Off the heat, beat in the butter and grated Parmesan to give a glossy thick paste. Season to taste. Pour the mixture into a lightly oiled shallow baking tin and spread to a thickness of about 1.5cm (½in). Allow to cool and set. Cut out rounds of polenta using a 2.5cm (1in) plain round cutter and dip into the egg and breadcrumbs to coat. Cover and chill until needed.

3 For the pea purée tip the peas and garlic into boiling water and cook for 2–3 minutes. Drain well and run under cold water to cool. Drain again. Pulse quickly in a blender with the mint and seasoning to form a coarse purée.

4 When ready to serve, heat the oil in a deep heavy-based pan or fryer to 190°C/375°F and fry the polenta in batches for 2–3 minutes until crisp and golden. Drain on kitchen paper. Use a teaspoon or piping bag to pipe on the purée. Top with a mint leaf, squeeze of lemon juice and a shaving of pecorino.

Busy mum's lifesaver I don't often serve deep-fried food but these really are worth the effort. If you don't have a thermometer, test the heat of the oil by dropping a small piece of bread into the hot fat. It should sizzle and brown quickly. However, the polenta pieces also cook quite well in the oven. Drizzle them with a little oil in a shallow tin and cook at 220°C/fan oven 200°C/ Gas Mark 7 for 10 minutes.

Alternative toppings:
● Asparagus and pesto ● Cooked chopped mushroom with truffle oil and tarragon
For non-vegetarians: ● Monkfish with cumin- and coriander-spiced polenta ● Sausage and tomato with sage, plus fried sage leaves

Green potato salad with avocado and basil

This salad is lovely warm or cold, and is ideal as part of a party table or stands as a great dish on its own – perfect! It's a family favourite when wonderful Jersey Royals are in season or for the first diggings of little potatoes from my vegetable beds.

Serves 4–6
Prepare 10 minutes
Cook 15 minutes

500g (1lb 2oz) small new potatoes, halved
2–3 sprigs fresh mint
2 cloves garlic, peeled
25g (1oz) pine nuts, toasted
3 tbsp grated pecorino (optional)
handful fresh basil leaves, shredded
3–4 tbsp extra-virgin olive oil
1 ripe avocado, peeled, stoned and diced
1 bunch spring onions, sliced
100g (4oz) fresh baby spinach, shredded
salt and freshly ground black pepper

1 Place the potatoes and mint in a pan, add water to just cover, bring to the boil and simmer for 12–15 minutes until tender. While the potatoes are cooking, work the garlic, pine nuts and seasoning to a coarse paste in a pestle and mortar or small food processor. Add the pecorino, if using, and basil and pound or process again until you have a coarse paste. Gradually beat in the olive oil a little at a time. Check the seasoning.

2 Drain the potatoes and toss with the basil pesto in a large bowl. Leave to cool. Stir the avocado, spring onions and spinach into the potatoes with seasoning and serve.

Busy mum's lifesaver Use readymade pesto to save time or try the pine nut and Parmesan dressing on page 194. For meat eaters serve with chicken or add cooked pancetta or smoked bacon cubes.

Double cooked goat's cheese and watercress soufflés

Soufflés are much easier to cook than you think – if you're worried then try this recipe. The soufflé mixture is cooked as usual but left to sink and cool. It is then turned out and baked again with a creamy sauce. A great starter for a party – or serve with salad leaves for a supper dish.

Serves 4
Prepare 20 minutes
Cook 25 minutes

50g (2oz) butter, melted, plus extra
    for brushing
50g (2oz) plain flour
300ml (½ pint) semi-skimmed milk
100g (4oz) goat's cheese (choose a
    good tangy one), crumbled
1 small bunch watercress, stalks
    discarded and leaves finely chopped
4 medium free-range eggs, separated
salt and freshly ground black pepper
4 tbsp double cream, to finish
3 tbsp freshly grated Parmesan,
    to finish

1 Preheat the oven to 200°C/fan oven 180°C/ Gas Mark 6. Use a little melted butter to brush the insides of 4 x 200ml (7fl oz) large teacups (don't use your best china!) or ramekins. Stir the flour into the remaining melted butter. Cook for a minute, then remove the pan from the heat and gradually whisk in the milk. Return the pan to the heat and stir until the sauce is very thick and smooth. Simmer for 2–3 minutes, stirring.

2 Remove the pan from the heat again and add the goat's cheese, watercress, egg yolks and plenty of seasoning. Whisk the egg whites until stiff but not dry and fold them quickly and lightly into the cheese base. Divide the mixture between the prepared cups or dishes and place on a baking sheet. Cook for 12–14 minutes until well-risen and golden. Remove from the oven and set aside to cool. They will sink down. Cover and chill until needed.

3 When ready to serve, carefully loosen the edges of the soufflés with a knife and turn them out into a buttered shallow ovenproof dish, leaving a space around each one. Spoon a tablespoon of cream over each soufflé and sprinkle with Parmesan. Return to the oven for 8–10 minutes until puffed up and heated through. Serve immediately.

Busy mum's lifesaver Add any flavour combinations you like to the basic mixture: for example, Stilton and walnut or spinach and Parmesan.

Moroccan filo pie

North African food frequently mixes sweet with savoury and the original dish that inspired this pie would be finished off with a dusting of icing sugar and cinnamon. But most people would expect a sweet interior with such a decoration, so I keep the spicing to the inside of the dish and omit the sugar and cinnamon dusting.

➡ Serve with the chickpea and apricot rice salad on page 70 or the lemon hollandaise on page 198.

Serves 6–8
Prepare 30 minutes
Cook 1 hour

1 large red pepper
150ml (¼ pint) hot water
15g (½oz) dried porcini mushrooms
5 tbsp olive oil
1 large onion, finely chopped
2 cloves garlic, finely chopped
¼ tsp saffron strands
1 tsp ground cinnamon
½ tsp each ground ginger and allspice
3 tbsp chopped fresh flat-leaf parsley
4 large free-range eggs, hard-boiled,
   shelled and chopped
50g (2oz) blanched almonds, toasted
230g (8oz) chestnut mushrooms,
   sliced
2 medium carrots, coarsely grated
1 bunch watercress, leaves finely
   chopped
7 sheets filo pastry
salt and freshly ground black pepper

1 Preheat the oven to 180°C/ fan oven 160°C/Gas Mark 4. Preheat the grill and cook the pepper on all sides until blackened. Place in a plastic bag for 2 minutes to loosen the skin. When cool enough to handle, skin, deseed and dice the pepper. Pour the hot water over the porcini and leave to stand for 15 minutes. Drain, reserving the liquid. Chop the mushrooms coarsely.

2 Heat 2 tbsp of the oil in a large frying pan, add the onion and garlic and cook for 5 minutes until softened and golden. Add the saffron and spices and cook for 30 seconds then add the parsley, mushroom liquid and seasoning, and simmer for 10 minutes until the liquid has almost evaporated. Stir in the chopped eggs and almonds. Season well.

3 Heat another tablespoon of the oil in a pan and add the porcini and chestnut mushrooms. Cook over a medium-high heat for 2–3 minutes then stir in the carrots, watercress and diced pepper and season to taste.

4 To assemble, brush 2 sheets of filo with oil and use to line a 23cm (9in) loose-bottomed cake tin, leaving the edges hanging over the side. Fold another sheet of filo in half and use to line the base. Spoon the onion and egg mixture over the pastry and cover with another sheet of filo. Add the mushroom mix and top with 2 more sheets of filo, tucking them down into the sides to create a neat parcel.

5 Brush the top of the pie with oil and decorate with the final sheet of filo crumpled into pieces. Bake for 40–45 minutes until golden and crisp. Transfer to a serving plate and serve.

Busy mum's lifesaver To make this dish for vegans use dried apricots instead of eggs – they accentuate the sweet and sour flavours. You need around 200g (7oz) soft apricots, roughly chopped. When working with filo pastry, stop it drying out by covering it with a damp tea towel and remove sheets as needed.

Italian rice and spinach cake

No one does formal entertaining any more, but it's still nice to bring something spectacular to the table occasionally. This luxurious but simple rice dish also makes a perfect party centrepiece, ready sliced into wedges. It's quite rich, so make sure you've got a sharp peppery salad to counteract it.

→ Serve with new potatoes – Jersey Royals in season – and a big salad.

Serves 4–6
Prepare 15 minutes
Cook 1 hour

350g (12oz) risotto rice
25g (1oz) butter
50g (2oz) freshly grated Parmesan
2 large free-range egg yolks
4 tbsp double cream
350g (12oz) fresh spinach
150g (5oz) buffalo mozzarella,
   roughly chopped
50g (2oz) pine nuts, toasted and
   coarsely chopped
1 shallot, finely chopped
freshly grated nutmeg
salt and freshly ground black pepper

1 Preheat the oven to 220°C /fan oven 200°C/Gas Mark 7. Cook the rice in plenty of boiling water for 10 minutes or until just tender. Drain thoroughly and mix with the butter, Parmesan and plenty of seasoning. Beat the egg yolks with the cream and stir into the rice.

2 Wash the spinach and cook in a covered pan with only the washing water clinging to its leaves, for 3–5 minutes until tender. Drain, pressing out any excess liquid, and chop finely. Mix with the mozzarella, pine nuts and shallot and season with nutmeg, salt and pepper.

3 To assemble, press half the rice mixture into a buttered deep 20cm (8in) loose-bottomed cake tin. Spoon the spinach mixture on top and spread level, then top with the rest of the rice. Press down firmly. Cover the tin with foil and bake for 45 minutes until set. Carefully turn out on to a plate and serve in wedges.

Leek and parsnip tarte tatin

Food writer Richard Cawley originally put the idea for this dish into my head with his description of a savoury version of tarte tatin made with parsnips. My recipe cuts up perfectly for nibbles with drinks; it also makes great picnic food and is ideal for a summer supper.

Serves 4
Prepare 20 minutes
Cook 35 minutes

175g (6oz) plain flour
½ tsp salt
large pinch of cayenne pepper
75g (3oz) butter
25g (1oz) freshly grated Parmesan
3 tbsp olive oil
450g (1lb) even-sized parsnips,
    thinly sliced
1 large leek, thickly sliced
1 tbsp clear honey
1 tbsp red wine vinegar
salt and freshly ground black pepper

1 Sift the flour, salt and cayenne into a bowl and rub in the butter until the mixture resembles breadcrumbs. Stir in the Parmesan and mix to a stiff dough with 2–3 tablespoons cold water. Knead lightly, then chill the pastry while you make the topping.

2 Preheat the oven to 200°C /fan oven 180°C/Gas Mark 6. Pour the oil into a deep 23cm (9in) flameproof gratin dish or ovenproof cast-iron frying pan and heat it directly on the hob. Arrange the parsnips and leek in a single layer over the surface, spoon over the honey and vinegar, then season. Cook gently for about 15 minutes, without turning or stirring the vegetables, until the parsnips are golden brown underneath and almost cooked through. Remove from the heat.

3 Roll out the pastry to around the same diameter as the gratin dish, carefully lift it over the vegetables and press firmly into place. Transfer the dish to the oven and bake for 20 minutes until the pastry is cooked through and golden.

4 Remove the tart from the oven and leave to stand for 5 minutes. Turn it out of the dish by placing a large serving plate on top and inverting both dish and plate, holding them firmly together, so the vegetables end up on top. Serve warm or cold.

Busy mum's lifesaver Use a 250g pack of readymade puff pastry as a quick alternative, but make sure you choose one made with butter for the best flavour.

Pine nut, caramelised red onion and rocket party pizza

This pizza goes down a storm at parties. It has no tomato sauce and can be made with or without cheese – perfect for catering for vegans. The oblong shape makes it easier to cut into squares for eating with fingers. Arrange the pizzas on slate tiles or square platters and then just cut them at the table for people to help themselves.

Makes 2 large pizzas (enough for 2–4 for supper or 6–8 at a party)
Prepare 15 minutes
Proving 1–1½ hours
Cook 35 minutes

500g (1lb 2oz) Italian 00 flour or
    strong white bread flour
1½ tsp salt
1 sachet easy-blend yeast
2 tbsp olive oil

For the topping
2 tbsp olive oil
3 large red onions, finely sliced
2 tbsp balsamic vinegar
50g (2oz) pine nuts
250g (9oz) buffalo mozzarella, torn
    into pieces (optional)
1 large bag wild rocket (about 200g)
salt and freshly ground black pepper

1 Sift the flour and salt into a mixing bowl and stir in the yeast. Whisk the oil with 300ml (¼ pint) warm water and add to the flour. Mix to a soft dough and turn on to a lightly floured work surface. Knead for 10 minutes until smooth and elastic. Place in a clean oiled bowl and cover with oiled cling wrap. Leave in a warm corner of the kitchen for 45 minutes or until doubled in size.

2 To make the onion topping, heat the oil in a large frying pan and add the onions. Cook very gently for about 10 minutes until really soft but not browned. Turn up the heat and stir for 2–3 minutes until the onions start to brown but take care they don't burn. Stir in the balsamic vinegar and pine nuts. Season to taste.

3 Preheat the oven to 220°C/fan oven 200°C/Gas Mark 7. Turn the dough out on to a floured surface and knead lightly to knock out any air. Divide into two and roll out to really thin oblongs about 2cm (¾in) thick. Transfer to floured baking sheets.

4 Spread the onion mixture over the dough, leaving a border round the edges, then scatter with the torn mozzarella if using. Cover with cling wrap and leave to sit again in a warm place for 15 minutes until puffy. Bake in the oven for 15–20 minutes until the top is golden and bubbling and the dough is crisp. Top with the rocket, drizzle with a little extra-virgin olive oil and seasoning and serve.

Busy mum's lifesaver For a party get ahead in one of two ways. For a really fresh pizza, make the dough ahead to step 3, roll out and chill it in the fridge, which will stop the yeast working. Then when you need it, just add the topping and leave to rise somewhere warm for 20–30 minutes. Or make the pizza and cook as above but don't add the rocket. Then when you need it, warm again in the oven and top with the rocket.

Summer vegetable platter with lemon chilli aioli

Seasonal young vegetables briefly blanched and arranged on a large platter with a spicy dip make great nibbles for a summer party. Or try giving them a blast on the barbecue to add a delicious charred flavour.

Serves 4–6
Prepare 15 minutes
Cook 10 minutes

4 tbsp extra-virgin olive oil
2 tbsp chopped fresh thyme
1.25kg (2½lb) mix of young top-quality
    vegetables, for example:
    courgettes, baby artichokes,
    asparagus tips, fennel, broad beans,
    carrots and baby cauliflower
coarse sea salt

For the lemon chilli aioli
½–1 medium red chilli, deseeded and
    chopped
2–3 cloves garlic, roughly chopped
1 free-range egg yolk
150ml (¼ pint) olive oil
grated rind and juice of ½ lemon
1 tsp smoked paprika
salt and freshly ground black pepper

1 Place the extra-virgin olive oil in a small pan with the thyme and warm the mixture gently for 2–3 minutes. Set aside to infuse. Trim all the vegetables and cut any large ones in half lengthways – the aim is to make sure they are easy to pick up and eat with your fingers. Cook the vegetables in batches in large pans of boiling water. The secret is to return the water to the boil fast after adding the veg, then simmer for 3–5 minutes, depending on the vegetable, until just tender. Drain thoroughly then toss with the infused oil.

2 Prepare the aioli. Place the chilli and garlic in a pestle and mortar and work to a paste or mash in a bowl with a fork. Work in the egg yolk and slowly drizzle in the olive oil a few drops at a time, whisking continuously, until the mixture thickens. Stir in the lemon juice, paprika and seasoning to taste. Transfer to a small serving bowl, cover and set aside.

3 Arrange the cooked vegetables on a platter, sprinkle with sea salt and serve with the aioli.

Busy mum's lifesaver You can't use a blender to make the aioli as there simply isn't enough volume – you'd end up trying to scrape it off the bowl and blades. So if you can't face making your own, buy a good-quality mayonnaise from the chiller cabinet and stir in a teaspoon of harissa paste. Or serve the veg with bowls of extra-virgin olive oil for dipping.

If you're handing round the veg as finger food, leave out the step with the infused oil or they'll be too slippery for guests to pick up!

Roasted vegetable terrine

This terrine is ideal for parties as it benefits from being made a day in advance to let the flavours develop. To create a really good flavour cook the aubergines and peppers until very soft and browned – this converts their natural sugars into caramel and transforms their flesh into melting softness. Take the terrine out of the fridge half an hour before serving to taste it at its best.

Serves 6
Prepare 30 minutes
Cook 45 minutes

5 tbsp olive oil, plus extra for brushing
2 medium aubergines, thinly sliced
    into rounds
2 yellow peppers
1 red pepper
3 medium courgettes, thinly sliced
    lengthways
8 baby leeks
175g (6oz) mascarpone cheese
1 clove garlic, crushed
1 tbsp black olive paste or sun-dried
    tomato paste
3 tbsp chopped fresh basil
400g can artichoke hearts, drained
salt and freshly ground black pepper

1 Preheat the oven to 220°C/fan oven 200°C/Gas Mark 7. Heat 4 tablespoons of the oil in a pan and fry the aubergine slices in batches until golden on both sides. Drain on kitchen paper. Place the peppers on a baking sheet and roast for 10–15 minutes until blackened. Place in a plastic bag and leave for 2 minutes for the skins to loosen. When cool enough to handle, skin, deseed and slice into thin strips.

2 Arrange the courgettes on a baking sheet with the leeks, brush with the remaining oil and season. Roast for 15–20 minutes until golden. While they are cooking beat the mascarpone with the garlic, olive or tomato paste, basil and seasoning.

3 Oil a 23cm x 13cm (9 x 5in) loaf tin and line the base and sides with the aubergine slices. Add a layer each of peppers, courgettes, leeks and artichokes, seasoning between each and pressing down, then add a layer of mascarpone mixture. Layer the remaining veg and mascarpone in the same way, finishing with a layer of aubergine slices. Cover the tin with plastic film and weight down with cans or weights. Chill overnight.

4 To serve the terrine, turn it out on to a serving plate and cut into thick slices with a sharp serrated knife or an electric carving knife.

Mozzarella peppers

A dish that's quick to prepare, beautiful to look at and delicious, so I make it again and again. Use multi-coloured peppers for a lovely centrepiece to a party spread and a mix of green and purple basil for an attractive finish. The recipe comes from a friend who now lives down under and I think of her every time I make this dish. It always gets a great response. Serve at room temperature for the best flavour.

➡ Serve with plenty of Italian bread such as ciabatta to mop up the juices.

Serves 6
Prepare 10 minutes
Cook 25 minutes

6 large peppers
4 tbsp olive oil
2 tbsp balsamic vinegar
3 cloves garlic, thinly sliced
3–4 tbsp extra-virgin olive oil
250g (9oz) buffalo mozzarella, sliced
salt and freshly ground black pepper
fresh basil leaves, to finish

1 Preheat the oven to 220°C/fan oven 200°C/Gas Mark 7. Cut the peppers in half from stem to tip and remove seeds and stem. Brush inside and out with oil. Place in a shallow baking tin in a single layer and cook in the oven for 20–25 minutes, turning over halfway through. The peppers should be tinged with black and just tender.

2 While the peppers are cooking, whisk the extra-virgin olive oil with the vinegar and seasoning and stir in the garlic. Remove the peppers from the oven and transfer to a serving platter. Spoon a little dressing into each pepper. Leave to cool to room temperature.

3 Just before serving place a slice or two of mozzarella in each pepper, top with basil and season.

Spiced chickpea and apricot rice salad

If, like me, you remember rice salads at parties as a child as depressingly dull, then this dish will change your mind. Though if you do end up with leftovers, be sure to keep them well chilled and don't store them for longer than 24 hours in the fridge – rice can be an ideal breeding ground for bugs if kept too long or at the wrong temperature.

Serves 6
Prepare 15 minutes
Cook 25 minutes

350g (12oz) basmati rice (or try
   brown rice)
1 tsp harissa paste
grated rind and juice of 2 limes
5 tbsp sunflower oil
4 tbsp chopped fresh coriander
100g (4oz) soft apricots, snipped
   into pieces
1 bunch spring onions, chopped
25g (1oz) pumpkin seeds or
   mixed seeds
400g can chickpeas, drained
salt and freshly ground black pepper
lime wedges, to serve

1 Cook the rice in a large pan of boiling water for 10 minutes until just tender. While the rice is cooking whisk the harissa, lime rind and juice, sunflower oil, coriander and seasoning together in a large mixing bowl. Drain the rice and run it under cold water, then drain really well again. Add to the dressing, stir and leave to cool.

2 Add the apricots, spring onions, seeds and chickpeas to the rice and stir to mix. Cover and chill for several hours to let the flavours develop. Serve with lime wedges.

Busy mum's lifesaver Try making this salad with cubed fresh mango instead of apricots. If you don't have harissa, use a medium curry paste instead.

the great outdoors

Many people look at you rather oddly if you start discussing vegetarian barbecues: I used to be one of them until I realised you can cook any vegetable on a barbecue and it tastes amazing.

My other barbecue 'moment' came when I bought a bucket barbecue from Rick Stein's shop in Padstow on a family holiday. Not only is it the best barbecue I've ever cooked on, it means you can up sticks to the beach (or the countryside) so easily and cook too. (That original bucket barbecue stood up to the task of cooking a huge barbecue for 12 hungry teenagers.) The recipes in this chapter can be cooked at home on any barbecue. I've also included instructions to adapt recipes to finish off the cooking in the open air. You'll find picnic dishes here, too, to prepare at home before you go out for the day. ➞

Barbecued asparagus with romesco sauce

We are used to steamed asparagus served with rich buttery sauces, but its distinctive flavour really comes out when cooked on the barbecue. This recipe is ideal for the first barbecue of summer or cooked on a portable one at a spring picnic, if we are lucky enough to have a few hot days in late May or June to coincide with the English asparagus season. It also cooks well under the grill.

→ Serve with lots of good sourdough bread to mop up any juices.

Serves 4
Prepare 15 minutes (including the sauce)
Cook 15 minutes

500g (1lb 2oz) fresh young asparagus
olive oil, for brushing
coarse sea salt
romesco sauce (see page 200)

1 Preheat the barbecue. Prepare the romesco sauce and transfer to a serving bowl.

2 Trim the asparagus, brush them with a little oil and cook on the barbecue for about 8–10 minutes, until tender. Turn the spears regularly and brush with a little more oil if they become too dry. Scatter with sea salt and serve with the sauce.

Busy mum's lifesaver Try serving barbecued asparagus with the pine nut and Parmesan dressing on page 194 or with scrambled eggs with a little grated Parmesan stirred into them.

Sweetcorn, courgette and mint tart

Home-made quiche is so much tastier and, on a picnic, the pastry doesn't go soggy like so many shop-bought versions. Now you can buy such good-quality readymade pastry it's reasonably quick to rustle one up before you set off. This recipe is a summertime family favourite.

→ Serve with a tomato and baby leaf salad.

Serves 6
Prepare 20 minutes
Cook 50 minutes

250g readymade all butter shortcrust pastry, defrosted if frozen
1 tbsp olive oil
1 red onion, finely chopped
3 small courgettes, trimmed and thinly sliced
200g can sweetcorn, drained
150ml (¼ pint) single cream
3 medium free-range eggs, beaten
2 tbsp chopped fresh mint
25g (1oz) grated Parmesan
salt and freshly ground black pepper

1 Preheat the oven to 200°C/fan oven 180°C/Gas Mark 6. Roll out the pastry into a circle about 1cm (¼in) thick and use to line a 23cm (9in) loose-bottomed flan tin. Fill the pastry case with crumpled greaseproof paper and dried rice or beans to hold it in place, and bake the pastry case 'blind' for 15 minutes. Remove the beans and paper.

2 While the pastry case is cooking heat the oil in a non-stick frying pan, add the onion and courgettes and cook for 5–6 minutes, turning the courgettes, until golden. Season and stir in the sweetcorn. Scatter over the base of the tart.

3 Beat together the cream, eggs, mint, Parmesan and seasoning. Pour over the vegetables and bake the tart for 25–30 minutes until puffy and golden brown. Serve warm or cold.

Spiced red bean koftas

These spiced patties are ideal candidates for cooking on the barbecue. My family loves them piled into warm Indian bread and topped with the hot mango and coconut chutney on page 201.

Serves 3–4
Prepare 20 minutes
Cook 10 minutes

400g can red kidney beans, well
    drained
1 tsp garam masala
½ tsp ground coriander
¼ tsp ground cumin
2 tbsp sunflower oil
1 small onion, finely chopped
1 clove garlic, finely chopped
½–1 green chilli, deseeded and
    chopped
salt and freshly ground black pepper

1 Place the beans in a bowl with the garam masala, coriander and cumin.

2 Heat the oil in a small frying pan and cook the onion, garlic and chilli for 3 minutes until the onion is softened. Add to the beans with plenty of seasoning and mash the ingredients together thoroughly. Shape the mixture into 16 small balls and thread them on to small wooden skewers, 2 per skewer. Chill until needed

3 To cook the koftas, place the skewers on the hot barbecue and cook for 6–8 minutes, turning regularly, until browned. Serve straight away.

Busy mum's lifesaver Soak wooden skewers in cold water for at least 30 minutes before use to prevent them burning. Be warned, if you use metal skewers the koftas will fall off as they cook – I'm talking from experience here.

Polenta and Parmesan wedges

Instant polenta is really easy to prepare, but watch out as it needs plenty of flavouring. Stirred through with Parmesan and fresh herbs, and studded with pine nuts and black olives, it becomes something else entirely, especially when cooked over coals to give it a delicious, earthy flavour and crisp exterior. These wedges will keep everyone going while you're cooking the rest of the barbecue.

→ Serve with the tomato chilli ketchup on page 201 or the lemon and walnut salsa verde on page 197.

Serves 4
Prepare 15 minutes
Cook 20 minutes

175g (6oz) instant polenta
15g (½oz) butter
25g (1oz) freshly grated Parmesan
3 tbsp chopped fresh basil
2 tbsp chopped flat-leaf parsley
8–10 black olives, stoned and
   chopped
25g (1oz) pine nuts, toasted
2 tbsp olive oil
salt and freshly ground black pepper

1 Preheat the barbecue. Bring 750ml (1¼ pints) water to the boil in a large saucepan. Add the polenta, stirring. Simmer over low heat for 5 minutes, stirring all the time, until the polenta is thick and comes away from the sides of the pan.

2 Stir in the butter, Parmesan, basil, parsley, olives and pine nuts and season to taste. Spoon the mixture into an oiled roasting tin and spread it out so that it's about 2.5cm (1in) thick. Leave to set for 10 minutes, then cut into triangles or wedges.

3 Brush the wedges with oil and cook them on the barbecue for 8–10 minutes, turning once or twice, until crisp and golden. Pile on to a warm serving platter.

Busy mum's lifesaver Make up double amounts of the polenta and freeze the wedges. Then just defrost and cook as needed. Try serving them with any of the vegetable stews such as the golden veg and bean stew on page 102.

Mushroom carrot burgers

These burgers are light and tasty and great cooked on the barbecue. I tend to steer clear of vegetables masquerading as meat dishes, but I make an exception when a particular combination works really well or, as here, is the logical way to cook a dish. Make sure you oil the grill so the burgers don't stick. → Serve with a leafy green salad.

Serves 4
Prepare 15 minutes
Cook 20 minutes

2 tbsp olive oil
1 medium onion, finely chopped
2 cloves garlic, finely chopped
350g (12oz) chestnut mushrooms, finely chopped
350g (12oz) carrots, grated
100g (4oz) fresh wholemeal breadcrumbs
75g (3oz) feta cheese
3 tbsp chopped fresh basil
2 tbsp chopped fresh thyme
2 medium free-range eggs, beaten
salt and freshly ground black pepper

1 Heat the oil in a large frying pan and add the onion and garlic. Cook for 3 minutes, until softened, but not browned. Stir in the mushrooms and cook over a medium heat for a further 5 minutes until soft.

2 Place the grated carrots in a large mixing bowl with the breadcrumbs. Crumble the feta into the mushroom mixture. Add the basil, thyme and plenty of seasoning. Beat the eggs and stir them in to bind the mixture.

3 Divide the mixture into four and pat into flat burgers. Use a fish slice or spatula to place the burgers on the barbecue and cook for 10–15 minutes, turning regularly, until the burgers are golden.

Busy mum's lifesaver Whiz up the onions, garlic and mushrooms in a processor or blender for speed, but don't overprocess them – you need some texture – then add the remaining ingredients.
   To freeze the uncooked burgers, place them on a baking sheet lined with baking parchment and open freeze for several hours. Then wrap tightly and label. Freeze for up to a month. To use, thaw thoroughly, then cook as above.

New potato and shallot kebabs with rocket pesto

Potatoes and onion are perfect partners – they feature together in dishes all over the world. I've used shallots here but the kebabs can also be made with quartered onions. Use metal skewers as they conduct the heat to the centre of the potatoes and ensure they cook through properly. I suggest marinating the vegetables for 30 minutes, but this can be reduced to 15 minutes if you are in a hurry.

Serves 4
Prepare 15 minutes plus standing time
Cook 30 minutes

500g (1lb 2oz) small new potatoes
8–10 shallots
1 clove garlic, finely chopped
1 tbsp olive oil
1 tsp grated lemon rind
12–16 fresh bay leaves
salt and freshly ground black pepper

For the pesto
25g (1oz) wild rocket
15g (½oz) walnut pieces
1 clove garlic
2 tbsp extra-virgin olive oil

1 Preheat the barbecue. Scrub the potatoes and cook in a medium saucepan of simmering water for 5 minutes. Add the shallots for the last 2 minutes. Drain the vegetables and peel the shallots, halving any large ones.

2 Mix together the garlic, oil, lemon rind and plenty of seasoning. Pour the mixture over the warm vegetables and leave them to stand for 30 minutes.

3 Meanwhile, place the rocket in a food processor or blender with the walnut pieces and garlic. Process until smooth, then gradually drizzle in the oil with the motor running to form a thick paste. Season to taste and transfer to a serving dish.

4 Thread the potatoes and shallots on to skewers with the bay leaves. Place the kebabs on the barbecue and cook for 15–20 minutes, turning occasionally and brushing with the marinade until golden and tender. Serve with the rocket pesto.

Busy mum's lifesaver Use shop-bought pesto if you are short of time but check that it's suitable for strict vegetarians. The kebabs go well with barbecued steak or sausages for meat eaters.

Chilled roasted tomato soup

I created this soup when I despaired of the flavour of British-grown summer tomatoes, as my family love chilled soups. Grilling or roasting really helps to bring out the taste, even when they're not at their best – it works for other veg too. When the weather warms up a chilled soup is a lovely way to cool down. Packed in a flask, it tastes even better outdoors.

Serves 4
Prepare 5 minutes
Cook 10 minutes

900g (2lb) large ripe tomatoes, halved
1 bunch spring onions, roughly
   chopped
2 large slices stale sourdough bread
2–3 cloves garlic, roughly chopped
1 tbsp sun-dried tomato paste
3 tbsp chopped fresh tarragon
1 tbsp red wine vinegar
600ml (1 pint) good-quality
   tomato juice
2–3 tbsp extra-virgin olive oil
salt and freshly ground black pepper
diced cucumber and red pepper,
   to serve

1 Preheat the grill. Grill the tomatoes skin-side down for 5 minutes until blackened then turn and cook the other side until the flesh is really soft. Scoop the flesh into a blender goblet and discard the skins.

2 Add the spring onions, bread, garlic, tomato paste, tarragon, vinegar, tomato juice and seasoning and process until smooth. Add 300ml (½ pint) iced water and the olive oil. Chill thoroughly.

3 Serve in chilled bowls or mugs with cucumber and pepper dice.

Busy mum's lifesaver To chill the soup in a hurry, add a couple of ice cubes to each serving.

Roasted pepper and mozzarella bruschetta

These open sandwiches with a distinctly Italian taste make a great starter at a barbecue. For a picnic I prepare the vegetables at home and pack them in a container, then toast the bread over the picnic fire (if there happens to be one) or use those little Italian paninis that come ready toasted. An open-crumbed bread such as ciabatta or a sourdough loaf soaks up the juices best.

Serves 4
Prepare 5 minutes
Cook 10 minutes

1 red pepper, halved and deseeded
1 yellow pepper, halved and deseeded
1 medium red onion, peeled and
   halved
3 tbsp good extra-virgin olive oil
3–4 tbsp chopped fresh oregano
2 cloves garlic, sliced (optional)
250g (9oz) mozzarella or goat's
   cheese, crumbled
4 large slices country-style bread
salt and freshly ground black pepper

1 Preheat the grill or barbecue. Grill the peppers and onion on both sides until blackened all over. Place the peppers in a plastic bag for 2 minutes for the skins to loosen. When cool enough to handle, skin and cut them into strips. Slice the onion.

2 Put the peppers and onion in a bowl with half the oil, the oregano, garlic if using and seasoning. Scatter over the cheese.

3 Toast the bread on both sides under the grill or over the barbecue and drizzle with the remaining oil. Top with the pepper mixture. Serve immediately.

Busy mum's lifesaver Use your best extra-virgin olive oil for bruschetta as the flavour makes all the difference. Try adding one shredded sun-dried tomato in oil to the mix, or 3–4 coarsely chopped black olives or capers, or a mixture of both.

Make sure you take plenty of napkins or wet wipes as the bruschetta are delicious but messy to eat.

Roasted aubergine and mint dip

This is my version of the classic Middle Eastern *baba ganoush,* also known as 'poor man's caviar'. Cooking the aubergine really well on the barbecue until it is soft and black intensifies its wonderful smoky flavour – it's irresistible.

→ Serve with vegetable sticks and fingers of pitta for dipping.

Serves 4
Prepare 15 minutes
Cook 15 minutes

2 medium aubergines
3 tbsp olive oil
½ tsp cayenne pepper
1 tsp ground cumin
1 clove garlic, crushed
juice of ½ lemon
2 tbsp chopped fresh mint
salt and freshly ground black pepper

1 Cut the aubergines in half from stalk to base. Slash the cut surfaces with a knife into a criss-cross pattern. Mix half the oil with the cayenne and cumin, and brush over the cut surfaces.

2 Place the aubergine halves on the barbecue, cut-side up, and barbecue for 10 minutes until really blackened. Turn and cook the other side until golden – the flesh must be really tender. Scrape the flesh into a blender or mixing bowl. Process or mash until smooth.

3 Add the garlic, then gradually add the lemon juice and remaining oil with the motor running, or while beating continuously by hand. Stir in the mint. Season to taste and transfer to a serving dish.

Busy mum's lifesaver The aubergines can be cooked in a hot oven instead of on a barbecue – at 220°C/fan oven 200°C/ Gas Mark 7 until the skins are really black. The recipe also works well with fresh coriander instead of mint and it can be transformed into a great salad by adding 2 deseeded and chopped tomatoes, 1 chopped red pepper and a finely chopped red onion. Pile it into ciabatta rolls – add some barbecued chicken for meat eaters.

Barbecued butternut squash with orange pecan butter

Squashes brushed with a flavoured butter and cooked over coals are a real treat: the sweetness of the flesh is enhanced by the flames. I've used butternut squash here, but you can substitute other varieties such as acorn squash or the little patty pans.

➡ Serve with a rice salad such as the one on page 70.

Serves 2–4
Prepare 5 minutes
Cook 20 minutes

1 butternut squash, about 750g (1¾lb) in weight
40g (1½oz) softened butter
grated rind and juice of ½ orange
few drops Tabasco
2 tbsp chopped fresh flat-leaf parsley
15g (½oz) pecan halves, finely chopped
salt and freshly ground black pepper

1 Preheat the barbecue. Place the whole squash in a pan of boiling water and simmer for 5 minutes. Drain and cut the squash in half from stalk to base and scoop out the seeds.

2 Beat the butter with the orange rind and juice, Tabasco, parsley and plenty of seasoning. Stir in the pecans.

3 Place the squash halves on the barbecue, cut-side down, and cook for 5 minutes. Turn the squash over and spread the flavoured butter over the cut sides. Cook for a further 8–10 minutes, until the flesh is tender and charred. Serve half per person for a main meal or cut into wedges as part of a general barbecue.

Sweet potatoes with quick curry crust and mango yogurt dip

I can think of no better way of cooking sweet potatoes than over hot coals. For this recipe, you simply slice them and brush the slices with a wonderful spicy paste. The whole process is simplicity itself and it intensifies the nutty flavour of the vegetable while cooking the outside to a crisp shell.

→ Serve with a green salad.

Serves 4
Prepare 10 minutes
Cook 20 minutes

750g (1¾lb) sweet potatoes
1 tbsp cumin seeds
1 tsp coriander seeds
½ tsp black peppercorns
1 tbsp smoked paprika
1 tsp cayenne
1 tbsp ground turmeric
salt
2 cloves garlic, roughly chopped
juice of 1 lemon
8 tbsp natural yogurt
2 tbsp mango chutney

1 Preheat the barbecue. Scrub the potatoes and cut into 1.5cm (½in) slices. Set aside. Heat a small frying pan till hot then add the cumin and coriander seeds and peppercorns and dry roast for 30 seconds.

2 Grind the roasted spices to a powder in a pestle and mortar or small grinder. Stir in the paprika, cayenne, turmeric and salt then add the garlic and a little lemon juice and pound the mixture to a paste. Stir this paste into half the yogurt with the rest of the lemon juice.

3 Pour the curry paste over the sweet potato slices and mix well until coated. Arrange the slices on the hot barbecue and cook for 15–20 minutes, turning regularly, until tender and golden. Serve at once with the remaining yogurt mixed with the mango chutney.

Busy mum's lifesaver This method also works well with other root vegetables, such as potatoes, swedes and turnips, but I suggest cooking them in boiling water for 5–8 minutes until nearly tender before draining and coating in the curry paste. Make up a jar of the paste and keep it in the fridge: it can be used in all kinds of dishes – meat eaters can use it on chicken or lamb. Or use a good-quality curry paste if you don't have all the spices.

Couscous salad with spiced barbecued vegetables

Brushing a spice-infused oil over the vegetables as they cook gives this salad an aromatic sweet-and-sour flavour, and it's so easy to make – just leave the oil to infuse while you prepare everything else.

➡ Serve piled into warm pitta bread with barbecued halloumi strips.

Serves 4
Prepare 20 minutes, plus 15 minutes
*   standing time*
Cook 15 minutes

230g (8oz) couscous
350ml (12fl oz) boiling vegetable stock
4 tbsp olive oil
½ tsp each ground cinnamon, ginger
    and smoked paprika
1 clove garlic, crushed
8 shallots
1 aubergine, thinly sliced lengthways
2 medium courgettes, thinly sliced
    lengthways
1 yellow pepper, halved and deseeded
1 tbsp balsamic vinegar
3 tbsp chopped fresh parsley
salt and freshly ground black pepper

1 Preheat the barbecue. Place the couscous in a bowl and pour in the stock. Leave to stand for 15 minutes, stirring occasionally. Gently warm the oil and spices in a small pan, then add the garlic and leave to infuse.

2 Place the shallots in a bowl, cover with boiling water and leave to stand for 5 minutes. Drain and peel the shallots, then thread them on to skewers.

3 Place all the vegetables on the barbecue and brush with the spiced oil. Cook for 10–15 minutes, turning and brushing with the oil, until tender and charred.

4 Remove the shallots from the skewer and cut in half. Cut the rest of the barbecued vegetables into thin strips. Add to the couscous with any remaining oil. Stir in the balsamic vinegar, parsley and seasoning. Serve warm or cold.

crowd pleasers

One of the beauties of veggie food is that it tends to be kinder on the purse when it comes to catering for the ravening hordes – I'm particularly thinking of teenagers here. The key is to buy food in season, and fill them up with plenty of complex carbohydrates such as lentils and beans. This has the added advantage of providing a good base for the kind of night out described by my dad as being 'on the toot'! Or simply a day of full-on beach or sporting activity. The dishes have been tested by my daughter Isobel on her student friends and even the comments from the meat-eating fraternity have been universally positive – they've all been asking for the recipes to get cooking themselves. ➞

Summer vegetable gratin

When summer vegetables are at their peak, they need little enhancement – the wonderful flavours work together to make a satisfying dish on their own. This recipe is a great way of using up a glut of home-grown courgettes: make as much as you need to, depending on how many people you're expecting to turn up.

→ Serve with plenty of crusty bread.

Serves 4–6
Prepare 15 minutes
Cook 30 minutes

750g (1¾lb) small to medium
   courgettes, thinly sliced
2 medium aubergines, thinly sliced
4 tbsp green pesto
3 tbsp extra-virgin olive oil
16 small (or cherry) tomatoes, sliced
40g (1½oz) fresh breadcrumbs
2–3 cloves garlic, chopped
3 tbsp chopped flat-leafed parsley
salt and freshly ground black pepper

1 Preheat the oven to 200°C/fan oven 180°C/Gas Mark 6. Place the courgettes and aubergines in a bowl and add the pesto, oil and seasoning. Toss together to coat, then arrange with the tomatoes in an oiled gratin dish large enough to take all the veg in a single layer.

2 Bake for about 20 minutes, basting with oil and juices, until the vegetables are golden.

3 Meanwhile, mix the breadcrumbs in a small bowl with the garlic and parsley. Remove the gratin from the oven and spoon the crumb mixture over the top, basting with any juices, then return the dish to the oven for a further 10 minutes until golden and the vegetables are tender.

Busy mum's lifesaver For big groups, double the quantities and cook in a deep roasting tin. The gratin also tastes great cold. To make it into a more substantial supper dish, add slices of mozzarella. Slice 100g (4oz) buffalo mozzarella cheese and tuck the slices between the vegetables. Add a couple more tablespoons of chopped fresh parsley to the topping and cook as above.

Braised aubergine red Thai curry

This dish is incredibly simple to prepare, cooks in no time and is just as good cold – in fact, I think it's one of the best recipes in the book. The sweet and sour Thai sauce really complements both the texture and smoky taste of the aubergines.

➡ Serve with Thai fragrant rice and shredded greens or spinach stir-fried with garlic and ginger.

Serves 6
Prepare 5 minutes
Cook 25 minutes

3 tbsp sunflower oil
2 medium onions, thinly sliced
3 cloves garlic, chopped
2.5cm (1in) piece fresh root ginger, peeled and finely chopped
2–3 tbsp medium curry paste
3 medium aubergines, cubed
juice of 1 lime
3 tbsp dark muscovado sugar
1 tbsp black bean sauce
salt
12–15 fresh basil leaves (use Thai basil if you can get it)

1 Heat the oil in a wok or large frying pan over a medium heat. Add the onions, garlic and ginger and stir-fry for 3 minutes until just beginning to brown. Stir in the curry paste and cook for 1 minute. Add the aubergine cubes and stir-fry for about 3–4 minutes until well browned.

2 Stir in the lime juice, sugar, black bean sauce, salt to taste and 600ml (1 pint) cold water and bring to the boil, stirring. Lower the heat, cover and simmer for 15 minutes until the aubergine is nearly tender.

3 Remove the pan lid and continue simmering the mixture until the liquid is reduced and the sauce is thick and syrupy. Serve immediately, scattered with basil.

Busy mum's lifesaver Readymade Thai curry pastes are generally not suitable for veggies as they contain fish sauce or shrimp paste; that's why I've used regular curry paste. Check labels to make sure you find a veggie one or make your own – there are several good recipes online.

Easy vegetable korma

Mild creamy sauces like this korma are the classic way to introduce children to curries – it's a favourite with mine. Balance the creaminess with a sharp dish such as the spinach and chickpea curry on page 30. → Serve with steamed rice and fresh chutney, such as the mango and coconut version on page 201.

Serves 6
Prepare 10 minutes
Cook 30 minutes

2 tbsp sunflower oil
1 large onion, thinly sliced
2.5cm (1in) piece fresh root ginger, roughly chopped
2–3 cloves garlic, finely chopped
2–3 tbsp medium curry paste
350g (12oz) vine tomatoes, quartered
500g (1lb 2oz) new potatoes, halved
1 medium butternut squash, peeled, deseeded and cut into chunks
400g can coconut milk
1 small cauliflower, cut into florets
juice of ½ lemon
1 tsp garam masala
3 tbsp chopped fresh coriander
salt and freshly ground black pepper

1 Heat the oil in a large heavy-based pan and add the onion. Fry over a medium heat for 6–8 minutes, stirring frequently until golden and soft. Stir in the ginger and garlic and cook for a minute, then add the curry paste and cook for a minute more. Add the tomatoes, potatoes and squash and stir to coat in the paste.

2 Add 200ml (7fl oz) cold water to the pan. Stir in the coconut milk then cover and simmer for about 20 minutes, stirring occasionally. About 5 minutes before the end of cooking, stir in the cauliflower and seasoning. Simmer until the vegetables are tender.

3 Stir in the lemon juice and garam masala and scatter with the chopped coriander.

Busy mum's lifesaver This dish is another catch-all for what is left in the vegetable drawer – courgettes, sweet potatoes, peppers, broccoli, anything that's to hand – and is an easy one for teenagers to rustle up for themselves. Buy a good-quality curry paste for the best results. To dress it up a bit, scatter the finished dish with toasted cashew nuts and browned sliced onions.

Spanish greens and rice stew with garlic chilli mayo

There is something indulgent and comforting about stirring a spoonful of garlicky mayo into the green depths of this stew. All the flavours meld and it smells heavenly. A pot on the stove is the ideal way to welcome all those hungry hordes after a weekend of sport or working outside.

⟶ Serve with crusty bread to mop up the juices.

Serves 4–6
Prepare 10 minutes
Cook 30 minutes

2 tbsp olive oil
2 large onions, finely chopped
3 medium turnips, peeled and diced
3 medium carrots, peeled and diced
500g (1lb 2oz) spring greens, shredded
¼ tsp saffron strands
1 litre (1¾ pints) hot vegetable stock
150g (5oz) risotto or paella rice
salt and freshly ground black pepper

For the mayo
2–3 cloves garlic
1 tsp smoked sweet paprika
1 small red chilli, deseeded and chopped
6 tbsp mayonnaise, ideally homemade with olive oil
juice of ½ lemon

1 Heat the oil in a large heavy-based pan and add the onions. Fry over a low heat for 3–5 minutes, stirring frequently until soft but not browned. Add the remaining vegetables and cook for a further 3–4 minutes until the greens wilt.

2 Mix the saffron strands with a couple of tablespoons of the hot stock then add to the vegetables with the remaining stock and seasoning. Bring to the boil and add the rice. Lower the heat and simmer for 15–20 minutes until the rice is tender.

3 While the stew is cooking pound the garlic in a pestle and mortar with the paprika and chilli to a paste. Gradually work in the mayonnaise and add lemon juice and seasoning to taste. Serve the stew in warm bowls with the mayo to stir in.

Busy mum's lifesaver I like spring greens in this dish but you can easily substitute kale, cavolo nero or spinach.

Risotto-stuffed peppers

On the whole I'm not a fan of stuffed veg – too many memories of dull watery courgettes or dry mushrooms from the 1970s. But these peppers are something different. Either make the risotto from scratch or use leftovers if you have some. You can use any pesto but I recommend a roasted pepper and chilli version for the best flavour.

→ Serve with a leafy salad and some Italian bread.

Serves 6
Prepare 15 minutes
Cook 35 minutes

6 large peppers, halved lengthways
    and deseeded
3 tbsp olive oil
1 medium onion, finely chopped
2 cloves garlic, chopped
250g (9oz) risotto rice
1 litre (1¾ pints) hot vegetable stock
5 tbsp good-quality pesto
4 tbsp freshly grated Parmesan
2 tbsp white breadcrumbs
salt and freshly ground black pepper

1 Preheat the oven to 190°C/fan oven 170°C/Gas Mark 5. Brush the pepper halves inside and out with a little oil and bake for 10 minutes, until just softened. Keep warm.

2 Meanwhile, heat the remaining oil in a medium pan and cook the onion and garlic for 3 minutes until softened. Add the rice and stir for a further minute. Keep the stock simmering in a pan. Add a ladleful of stock to the pan and simmer over a medium-low heat until the liquid is absorbed, stirring. Continue adding the stock, a ladleful at a time, stirring until it has been absorbed, before adding the next lot. Carry on until all the stock is absorbed and the rice is tender and creamy but still with a slight bite. This should take about 20 minutes. Stir in the pesto and season to taste.

3 Pile the rice into the pepper halves, sprinkle with Parmesan and breadcrumbs and heat in the oven for 8–10 minutes until piping hot.

Roasted aubergine and tomato pasta cake

This spectacular dish looks impressive, can be made well in advance and then heated through. And it's easy to eat with a fork – always a bonus if you're cooking for a crowd. It originates from Sicily, where aubergines, tomatoes and fresh basil are ubiquitous. Make sure you cut the aubergine into thin slices as you use them to line a deep tin – if they're too thick, they won't be flexible enough.

→ Serve with a green salad.

Serves 6
Prepare 30 minutes
Cook 1 hour

4 tbsp olive oil
2 cloves garlic, chopped
4 tbsp chopped fresh basil
1 tsp crushed dried chilli
400g can chopped Italian tomatoes
sunflower oil, for frying the aubergines
2 large aubergines, thinly sliced into
    rounds
450g (1lb) penne pasta
50g (2oz) stoned black olives,
    chopped
150g (5oz) mozzarella, grated
25g (1oz) freshly grated Parmesan
1 tsp dried oregano
salt and freshly ground black pepper

1 Preheat the oven to 200°C/fan oven 180°C/Gas Mark 6. Heat half the oil in a medium pan, add the garlic, basil and chilli and cook over a high heat for 1 minute until golden. Stir in the tomatoes and seasoning and simmer for 20–25 minutes until thickened.

2 Meanwhile, heat about 2.5cm (1in) sunflower oil in a deep frying pan and fry the aubergine slices in batches until golden. Drain on kitchen paper. Cook the pasta in plenty of boiling salted water for 8–10 minutes or according to pack instructions. Drain and toss with the remaining oil. Mix the pasta with the tomato sauce, olives, cheeses, oregano and seasoning.

3 Line the base and sides of a greased, spring-release 20cm (8in) cake tin with the aubergine slices, then spoon the pasta mixture into the centre. Arrange the rest of the aubergine slices on top and press down firmly. Bake for 25 minutes until piping hot. Turn out on to a warm serving dish and cut into wedges.

Busy mum's lifesaver Keep any leftovers in the fridge and serve them cold or pack up for a picnic.

Vegetable biryani with crispy onions

A biryani is a great choice if you suddenly have to cook for large numbers of people at the last minute, as you can use any seasonal vegetables that you have to hand. I cook it in a heavy-duty roasting tin on the hob, cover it with foil and then it can sit in a low oven until needed.

➡️ Serve with the cucumber and walnut raita on page 196 and a selection of chutneys.

Serves 6
Prepare 10 minutes
Cook 40 minutes

3 tbsp sunflower oil
3 medium carrots, scrubbed and
   thickly sliced
3 medium parsnips, peeled and
   thickly sliced
3 medium onions, thinly sliced
1 medium cauliflower, cut into florets
150g (5oz) green beans, trimmed
350g (12oz) basmati rice
3 tbsp biryani paste
400g can chopped Italian tomatoes
1 litre (1¾ pints) vegetable stock
salt and freshly ground black pepper
toasted flaked almonds, raisins and
   fresh coriander, to garnish

1 Preheat the oven to 190°C/fan oven 170°C/Gas Mark 5. Heat 2 tablespoons of the oil in a large shallow flameproof casserole or roasting tin over a medium heat. Add the carrots, parsnips and half the onions, and cook for 5 minutes, stirring, until lightly browned. Stir in the cauliflower and beans and cook for a minute or two.

2 Stir in the biryani paste and rice and cook for 1 minute. Add the tomatoes, stock and seasoning. Bring to the boil, cover and transfer to the oven for 25–30 minutes until the stock is absorbed.

3 While the rice and vegetables are cooking, heat the remaining oil in a shallow frying pan and cook the remaining onions over a low heat for 10 minutes until really soft but not browned. Turn up the heat and cook for a few more minutes until golden brown and crisp. Take the biryani out of the oven, fork through the rice and garnish with the fried onions, almonds, raisins and fresh coriander.

Busy mum's lifesaver If you have time, soaking the basmati rice before cooking produces a lighter, less sticky grain. Just rinse the rice in a sieve until the water runs clear, then soak it in plenty of cold water for about 30 minutes. Drain and use as directed in the recipe.

Hearty spiced lentil and cauliflower soup

A big pot of soup on the stove is perfect food for hungry young people. Mugs of soup on a cold night with some bread and maybe a dip or two are a good way of filling them up before a night out.

→ Serve with warm naan bread.

Serves 6
Prepare 15 minutes
Cook 35 minutes

2 tbsp groundnut oil
1 medium onion, chopped
2 sticks celery, chopped
1 medium carrot, diced
1 red chilli, deseeded and finely
   chopped
1 tsp ground cumin
2–3 cloves
½ tsp ground turmeric
100g (4oz) red lentils
1.5 litres (2½ pints) vegetable stock
1 medium cauliflower, cut into florets
1 tsp black mustard seeds
2 cloves garlic, very thinly sliced
salt and freshly ground black pepper

1 Heat half the oil in a large pan and add the onion, celery and carrot. Cook for 3–4 minutes until soft. Add the chilli, cumin, cloves and turmeric and cook for a further minute, then stir in the lentils. Pour in the stock and continue cooking for 15 minutes. Add the cauliflower and simmer for a further 10–15 minutes until tender.

2 Remove three or four of the cauliflower florets, break them into small pieces and keep aside. Blend the soup in a processor or blender until smooth, then return to the pan. Check the seasoning and reheat, but don't let it boil.

3 Heat the remaining oil in a small frying pan and add the mustard seeds and garlic. Cook for 30 seconds then add the reserved cauliflower and allow to brown. Pour the soup into warm mugs or bowls and add a little of the cauliflower garnish.

Busy mum's lifesaver Use 650g (1¼lb) frozen cauliflower florets instead of the fresh for convenience. This soup freezes well so make up a big batch and freeze it in small blocks.

Rice noodles with green beans, coconut and mango

A family favourite, this soup-style noodle dish is a classic combination of sweet and sour flavours. I like to use rice noodles for their fine texture – all you need to do is soak them in boiling water. But it works just as well with thin egg noodles. Make sure you use a good-quality curry paste for the best results.

Serves 6
Prepare 10 minutes
Cook 15 minutes

2 tbsp sunflower oil
2 medium red onions, sliced
2–3 cloves garlic, chopped
2–3 tbsp curry paste
300ml (½ pint) vegetable stock
400ml can coconut milk
350g (12oz) rice noodles
300g (10oz) green beans, trimmed
2 red peppers, deseeded and
    thinly sliced
1 large ripe mango, peeled, stoned
    and cubed
salt and freshly ground black pepper
chopped fresh coriander, to garnish

1 Heat the oil in a large pan or wok. Add the onions and garlic and cook for 5 minutes until golden. Stir in the curry paste and cook for a minute. Add the stock, coconut milk and seasoning. Allow to simmer for 5 minutes.

2 Place the noodles in a bowl and pour over boiling water. Leave to stand for 5 minutes then drain. Cook the green beans in boiling water for 3–4 minutes until just tender, then drain.

3 Add the hot noodles and beans to the coconut liquid and spoon into serving bowls. Arrange the peppers and mango on top. Garnish with coriander and serve.

Busy mum's lifesaver Add cubes of salmon fillet to this dish for fish eaters. Fry 350g (12oz) cubed salmon with the curry paste in step 1 and continue as above.

Golden veg and bean stew with garlic flat bread

This fresh-tasting, colourful stew is just the thing to serve on a late summer or early autumn day, when pumpkins are beginning to appear in the shops. A medium pumpkin should give the correct amount of flesh and will be sweeter and more tender than some of the monsters on sale.

→ Serve with garlic flat bread (see below).

Serves 4–6
Prepare 20 minutes
Cook 40 minutes

3 tbsp olive oil
1 large onion, finely chopped
2 leeks, sliced
2 garlic cloves, chopped
2 sticks celery, sliced
150g (5oz) small carrots
1 medium swede, peeled and cut into chunks
2 parsnips, peeled and cut into chunks
230g (8oz) new potatoes, halved if large
350g (12oz) pumpkin flesh, cut into 2.5cm (1in) chunks
2 tbsp sun-dried tomato paste
1 litre (1¾ pints) vegetable stock
2 x 400g cans borlotti beans, drained
salt and freshly ground black pepper

1 Heat the oil in a large flameproof casserole. Add the onion, leeks and garlic and cook for 5 minutes until softened. Add the remaining vegetables and cook for 8–10 minutes, stirring occasionally until they are just turning golden.

2 Add the tomato paste, stock, borlotti beans and plenty of seasoning. Bring to the boil and simmer for 20–25 minutes until the vegetables are tender. Serve with the flat bread.

Busy mum's lifesaver Make this great flat bread and you'll really transform the dish. Make up half the amount of pizza dough on page 64 or use a packet bread mix. Roll out the proved dough into thin circles, place on baking sheets and slash across the centre with a knife at intervals to make cuts. Bake for 15 minutes at 220°C/fan oven 200°C/Gas Mark 7. While the bread is cooking mix together 2 tbsp olive oil and 2 chopped cloves garlic. Spoon over the warm bread as it comes out of the oven and serve scattered with coarse salt.

New potato and spring-green hash

Dark leafy vegetables have a sorry place in the history of British cookery – the aroma of overcooked cabbage used to be a feature of all too many school dining rooms. So Spain is the inspiration for this recipe – the Spanish have the knack of taking a few ingredients and making a simple dish of intense flavours that is very satisfying both to cook and to eat. You can make it with chard or kale and it's an easy dish to scale up or down depending on numbers.

→ Serve with plenty of crusty bread.

Serves 3–4
Prepare 10 minutes
Cook 30 minutes

4 tbsp olive oil
450g (1lb) new potatoes, thinly sliced
1 medium red onion, sliced
350g (12oz) spring greens or Savoy
   cabbage, shredded
1 clove garlic, crushed
1 dried chilli, chopped
3–4 medium free-range eggs
salt and freshly ground black pepper

1 Preheat the oven to 200°C/fan oven 180°C/Gas Mark 6. Heat 3 tablespoons of the oil in a large frying pan until very hot, then add the potatoes and onion a few slices at a time to prevent them sticking together, seasoning each layer well. Cook over a medium heat for about 10 minutes, turning occasionally, until the potatoes are golden and tender.

2 Meanwhile, bring a large pan of water to the boil, add the greens and cook for 2 minutes until just wilted. Drain and pat dry with kitchen paper. Heat the remaining tablespoon of oil in a medium pan, add the garlic and chilli and cook for 1 minute until golden. Add the greens and seasoning and stir over a medium heat for 3–4 minutes until just browned. Take care they don't burn.

3 Mix the greens with the potatoes and transfer to a shallow earthenware casserole. Make three or four slight indentations in the top and break an egg into each one. Bake for 8–10 minutes until the eggs are just set, then serve immediately.

Busy mum's lifesaver Prepare the veg in advance and add the eggs later, but reheat the veg in the oven before you add the eggs. For big groups, double up the quantities and cook in a deep roasting tin.

Roasted pepper and white bean hotpot

This dish is comforting and filling and great for student gatherings – it's the next step up from baked beans. If I have them to hand I use wonderful Spanish *alubia* beans for their great texture, but cannellini beans will do fine.

➡ Serve with bread and a large salad.

- -

Serves 6–8
Prepare 10 minutes
Cook 30 minutes

3 large peppers, red, yellow or orange
2 tbsp olive oil
1 large onion, finely chopped
3 cloves garlic, finely chopped
300ml (½ pint) red wine
400g can Italian chopped tomatoes
1 tbsp smoked paprika
2 tbsp chopped fresh thyme
3 x 400g cans cannellini beans,
 drained
salt and freshly ground black pepper
chopped flat-leaf parsley, to garnish

1 Preheat the grill. Place the peppers underneath and cook on all sides until blackened. Place them in a bag for 5 minutes to soften, then peel off and discard the skins. Deseed the peppers and roughly chop the flesh.

2 Heat the oil in a large saucepan and add the onion and garlic. Cook over a medium heat for 3 minutes until softened. Stir in the red wine and boil for a minute or two to cook off the alcohol. Add the tomatoes, smoked paprika, thyme and seasoning and simmer gently for 15 minutes to thicken the sauce.

3 Add the beans and grilled peppers and simmer for a further 10 minutes, stirring occasionally until thick and piping hot. Check the seasoning and scatter with chopped parsley. Serve in warm bowls.

Busy mum's lifesaver Use chickpeas or borlotti beans instead if you don't have cannellini beans to hand. This also makes a good sauce for pasta, with or without beans. If I'm in a rush, I use a jar of ready-grilled peppers.

food to go

The packed-lunch blues were a regular feature of school mornings in our household until I worked out a strategy. I found doubling up to be the best technique: cooking something for supper the night before that, with a few additions, can morph into a delicious packed lunch the next day. Of course, it's not just children who take packed lunches: if you're on a budget or work in an area with few snack bars, or if you're going on a train journey and don't want to pay inflated prices, you'll appreciate these ideas. All dishes taste good warm or cold and they work well together, so that you can mix and match them to make up a more substantial lunch. Work colleagues or fellow travellers will be craning their necks to see what you're tucking into. My stepson Henry was a willing tester for these recipes while he was on sixth-form work experience. His feedback? Pack larger quantities, include some wet wipes, and have food on standby for when he gets home – luckily these recipes are good for grazing straight from the fridge, too. →

Spinach, pine nut and ricotta filo pinwheels

These Greek-inspired pinwheels are wonderful served hot or cold. Cook them all together, then split them apart and wrap individually in foil for packed lunches. If you want to take them on a picnic, transport them in the cake tin you baked them in and divide them up when you arrive.

Serves 4
Prepare 10 minutes
Cook 35 minutes

250g (9oz) fresh baby spinach
1 tbsp sunflower oil
1 red onion, sliced
1 clove garlic, crushed
50g (2oz) pine nuts, toasted
freshly grated nutmeg
4 sheets filo pastry
melted butter, for brushing
200ml carton ricotta
1 tbsp sesame seeds
salt and freshly ground black pepper

1 Preheat the oven to 200°C/fan oven 180°C/Gas Mark 6. Wash the spinach and place in a pan with just the water clinging to the leaves, season, cover the pan and cook for 3–4 minutes until tender. Drain thoroughly and squeeze out any excess water. Heat the oil in a frying pan, add the onion and garlic and cook for 3 minutes until softened. Add the pine nuts and cook for a minute or two until golden, then stir in the spinach. Season with salt, pepper and nutmeg.

2 Cut the sheets of filo in half and brush with melted butter. Spread the spinach mixture over the bottom third of each rectangle. Scatter with ricotta then roll up from the short side tucking in the sides as you go, to form a long cigar shape. Brush the outside of the cigar-shaped roll with butter, then coil it into a pinwheel and tuck it into a buttered 20cm (8in) loose-bottomed cake tin. Repeat with the remaining spinach mixture, ricotta and filo pastry, arranging them round the edge of the tin, with one in the middle.

3 Brush the top of the filo wheels with melted butter and scatter with sesame seeds. Bake for 20–25 minutes until golden and crisp.

Chickpea, rocket and pepper tortilla

Make a big tortilla for supper and with any luck you'll have some leftovers to slice up for packed lunches or picnics – they're also excellent cut into cubes and served as an appetiser with drinks.

Serves 3–4
Prepare 10 minutes
Cook 20 minutes

1 yellow pepper
4 tbsp olive oil
1 medium onion, sliced
2 medium potatoes, cooked in their
   skins and thickly sliced
50g (2oz) canned chickpeas
50g (2oz) wild rocket
5 large free-range eggs
salt and freshly ground black pepper

1 Preheat the grill. Grill the pepper under a high heat until blackened on all sides, then place in a plastic bag for 5 minutes for the skin to loosen. Peel off and discard the skin, deseed the pepper and cut into strips.

2 Heat half the oil in a frying pan, add the onion and potatoes, seasoning well, and cook for 8–10 minutes until golden. Add the chickpeas, pepper strips and rocket and continue cooking for a couple of minutes to heat through. Drain the vegetables in a sieve. Beat the eggs in a bowl, add the drained vegetables and stir to combine. Leave to stand for 5 minutes.

3 Heat the remaining oil in a 20cm (8in) non-stick frying pan, add the egg mixture and cook over a low to medium heat for 5–8 minutes until the egg is set on top and golden underneath. Place a large plate over the pan and very carefully invert the frying pan to tip the tortilla out on to the plate, cooked-side upwards. Carefully slide it back into the pan for 5 minutes to cook the other side. Repeat twice to give the tortilla its traditional cake shape.

Busy mum's lifesaver Use char-grilled peppers from a jar when in a hurry. Try making the tortilla with sweet potato instead for a change.

Falafel in pitta pockets with tahini dressing

These spicy little patties make an ideal packed lunch tucked inside pitta pockets. You can also serve them at home as part of a satisfying mezze-style spread, along with the couscous salad with barbecued vegetables on page 88 and the roasted aubergine and coriander dip on page 84.

Serves 4
Prepare 20 minutes
Cook 6 minutes

2 x 400g cans chickpeas, drained
50g (2oz) fresh wholemeal
    breadcrumbs
2 cloves garlic, finely chopped
1 small red chilli, deseeded and
    chopped
1 stick celery, sliced
2 spring onions, sliced
2 tsp ground cumin
2 tsp ground coriander
¼ tsp turmeric
2 tbsp olive oil
salt and freshly ground black pepper
pitta bread, to serve

For the yogurt dressing
6 tbsp Greek-style yogurt
2 tbsp chopped fresh mint
1–2 tbsp tahini paste

1 Place the chickpeas in a food processor with the breadcrumbs, garlic, chilli, celery and spring onions and process until smooth. Then add the cumin, coriander, turmeric, olive oil and salt to taste. Process again. Shape the mixture into eight small patties and chill them for 15 minutes.

2 Stir the yogurt and mint into the tahini for the dressing and season to taste.

3 Preheat the grill. Place the falafel directly on the grill pan (they'll fall through the rack) and cook for 3 minutes on each side, until golden. Warm the pittas, cut them in half and open into pockets. To serve hot, slip a couple of falafel into each pitta pocket and drizzle in a little of the dressing. For a packed lunch tuck the cold falafel into the pittas and pack the dressing separately in a little pot.

Puy lentil salad with feta, lemon and green beans

If you keep a bowlful of lentils in the fridge you've always got the makings of food to go. This salad is a family favourite – we like it piled into pitta bread with a dollop of the chickpea hummus on page 115.

Serves 4
Prepare 10 minutes
Cook 20 minutes

350g (12oz) green beans, topped and tailed
grated rind and juice of 1 lemon
3 tbsp extra-virgin olive oil
1 clove garlic, crushed
200g (7oz) Puy lentils
2 bay leaves
25g (1oz) walnut pieces, roughly chopped
25g (1oz) pumpkin seeds
6 spring onions, sliced
100g (4oz) Greek feta, cubed
salt and freshly ground black pepper

1 Cook the beans in boiling water for 3–4 minutes until just tender. Drain and run under cold water to cool. Drain again. Whisk the lemon juice, oil and garlic with seasoning in a mixing bowl and add the drained beans. Toss to coat in the dressing.

2 Place the lentils and bay leaves in a pan with enough cold water to cover generously. Bring to the boil and simmer for 15 minutes until just tender. Drain and remove the bay leaves. Cool for 5 minutes or so then add to the beans.

3 Add the walnuts, pumpkin seeds, spring onions and feta. Toss gently together and serve.

Busy mum's lifesaver This salad tastes best served at room temperature so get it out of the fridge or lunch box ahead to enjoy it at its best. You can use precooked sachets of lentils for speed but remember they do work out much more expensive.

Curried pumpkin soup

A flask of soup is a welcome addition to a lunch box on a cold day. And this really simple warming soup is just the thing to make at Hallowe'en, as it uses up the insides of those endless pumpkin lanterns children like to make. A pumpkin weighing just under a kilo (2¼lb) will yield the right weight of flesh.
➡ Serve with crusty bread.

Serves 4
Prepare 10 minutes
Cook 25 minutes

450g (1lb) pumpkin flesh, cubed
230g (8oz) celeriac, peeled and cubed
1.5 litres (2½ pints) vegetable stock
1 tbsp good-quality curry paste
25g (1oz) butter, diced (optional)
salt and freshly ground black pepper

1 Place the pumpkin, celeriac and stock in a large saucepan, stir in the curry paste and seasoning and bring to the boil. Simmer for 20 minutes or until the vegetables are tender.

2 Process the soup in a blender or food processor until smooth, then return it to the pan and reheat until almost boiling. Gradually whisk in the butter, if using, until completely incorporated. Serve immediately.

Busy mum's lifesaver Freeze the soup before you add the butter. Recycle shop-bought pasta sauce cartons – they're ideal for freezing in individual portions. For vegans, leave out the butter and add a swirl of chilli oil at the end. Any other squash will do, such as butternut or the turban-shaped kabocha.

Spring onion, tomato and chickpea hummus

It's always a good idea to keep some kind of hummus on standby in the fridge – then you've got the makings of a packed lunch or quick snack. This version is so simple and fast to make and can be served on its own as a dip or with the falafel on page 112 and the lentil salad on page 113.

➡ Serve with pitta bread and/or vegetable crudités for dipping.

Serves 4
Prepare 10 minutes
Cook 15 minutes

400g can chickpeas, drained
1 tsp sun-dried tomato paste
½ tsp ground cumin
½ tsp smoked paprika
1–2 cloves garlic, crushed
juice of 1 large lemon
2 tbsp extra-virgin olive oil, plus extra
6–8 spring onions, finely chopped
salt and freshly ground black pepper
chopped flat-leaf parsley, to serve

1 Place the chickpeas in a processor or blender with the tomato paste, cumin, paprika, garlic, lemon juice and seasoning and whiz until almost smooth. Add the oil and blend again quickly. Transfer to a bowl and stir in two thirds of the chopped spring onions.

2 Scatter with the remaining chopped onion, chopped parsley and a drizzle of olive oil.

Patatas bravas

Once again I return to Spain for inspiration – these potatoes are a delicious tapa and also make a great base for a packed lunch. If you're eating them at home, they taste good hot or cold.

⟶ Serve with bread and olives.

Serves 4
Prepare 10 minutes
Cook 35 minutes

500g (1lb 2oz) large new potatoes, scrubbed
4 tbsp olive oil
1 small onion, finely chopped
1 clove garlic, crushed
½ tsp dried chilli flakes
230g (8oz) tomato passata
6 tbsp dry white wine
3 tablespoons chopped flat-leaf parsley, plus extra, to serve
salt and freshly ground black pepper
½ teaspoon smoked paprika

1 Place the potatoes in a saucepan of cold water and bring to the boil. Cook for 10–12 minutes, until the potatoes are almost tender.

2 Meanwhile, heat a tablespoon of the oil in a small saucepan and add the onion and garlic. Cook for 3–4 minutes, until softened, then stir in the chilli, passata, wine, parsley and seasoning. Simmer for 20 minutes until thickened, stirring occasionally.

3 Drain the potatoes and refresh them under cold water. Pat dry and cut each one into four wedges. Heat the remaining oil in a large non-stick frying pan and cook the potatoes on all sides over a medium heat until golden. Sprinkle over the paprika, pour over the tomato sauce and serve scattered with extra parsley.

Busy mum's lifesaver For a perfect packed lunch put the potatoes into a container with some cubes of feta and the lentil salad on page 113. If catering for meat eaters too, add cubed chorizo, quickly fried when you fry the potatoes – fry half the potatoes with meat and half without.

Indonesian vegetable salad with peanut dressing

The peanut sauce transforms this salad and the contrast between the crunchy veg and spicy sweet and sour dressing is very satisfying. Vary the veg you use depending on what you have to hand – I recommend all kinds of beans and peas, peppers, broccoli or strips of courgette. Pack salad and dressing separately for best results.

Serves 2–3
Prepare 10 minutes
Cook 15 minutes

175g (6oz) small new potatoes
1 medium carrot, cut into matchsticks
175g (6oz) fine green beans, trimmed
175g (6oz) white cabbage, shredded
100g (4oz) fresh bean sprouts
¼ cucumber, cut into matchsticks

For the peanut sauce
1 tsp sunflower oil
1 clove garlic, finely chopped
4 tbsp crunchy peanut butter
1 tbsp soy sauce
1 tsp dark muscovado sugar
1 tbsp lemon juice
1 tbsp hot chilli sauce
4 tbsp coconut milk

1 Make the peanut sauce. Heat the oil in a small pan over a medium heat. Add the garlic and cook for 1 minute until golden. Stir in the peanut butter and 4 tablespoons cold water and mix. Off the heat, stir in the soy sauce, sugar, lemon juice and chilli sauce, then return the pan to the heat and simmer, stirring, to give a fairly smooth sauce. Stir in the coconut milk and heat through. Set aside.

2 Bring two saucepans of water to the boil. Add the potatoes to one and cook for 10–12 minutes until tender. Add the carrot and green beans to the other pan, return to the boil and cook for 3 minutes, adding the cabbage for the last minute – the vegetables should still be crisp. Drain all the vegetables, refresh under cool water and drain again. Pat dry with kitchen paper.

3 Place the cooked vegetables in a large bowl, add the bean sprouts and cucumber and gently toss together. If eating at home, pour the peanut sauce over the salad and serve.

Busy mum's lifesaver You can dress this salad in advance and pack it into lunch boxes, but keeping the dressing separate and pouring it on to the salad just before eating keeps the flavours fresh. I collect little pots for this very purpose – pots that readymade pesto came in, for example – and nag to make sure people bring them back so I can use them again and again.

Courgette, black olive and feta tarts

Hurray for readymade pastry with butter. The flavour is so good and it means these little open tarts are a doddle to make, especially if you really cheat and use the ready-rolled sheets as I've done here. Individual tarts make a neat packed lunch.

→ Serve with a leafy salad.

Serves 3–4
Prepare 20 minutes
Cook 30 minutes

1 sheet puff pastry made with butter
3 tbsp sun-dried tomato paste
100g (4oz) feta, cubed
50g (2oz) black olives, stoned and
   halved
200g (7oz) baby courgettes, trimmed
1 tbsp olive oil
1 tbsp chopped fresh rosemary
salt and freshly ground black pepper

1 Preheat the oven to 200°C/ fan oven 180°C/Gas Mark 6. Cut the pastry sheet into four squares. Form a border by making a shallow cut 1.5cm (½in) in from the edge all around each square, without actually cutting through the pastry. Arrange the pastry squares on a damp baking sheet.

2 Spread half the sun-dried tomato paste over each square of pastry, leaving the border clear. Scatter over the feta and olives. Cut the courgettes in half lengthways. Mix together the remaining tomato paste, olive oil and seasoning and toss with the courgettes. Arrange the courgettes in lines on top of the feta and olives. Scatter with the rosemary and bake for 25–30 minutes until the pastry is cooked through and crisp. Serve warm at home or leave to cool and wrap up for food on the go.

Vegetable empanadas

These little pasties come from Spain. Fill them with this mixture of sweet potato and green pepper, which really picks up the lovely flavour of the sweet paprika – they are so moreish. The pasties freeze well: make a big batch then you can defrost them individually the night before, all ready to slip into lunch boxes next morning.

Makes 15
Prepare 30 minutes
Cook 35 minutes

200g (7oz) plain flour
1 tsp baking powder
¼ tsp salt
25g (1oz) butter, cubed
25g (1oz) white vegetable fat, cubed
1 medium free-range egg, beaten
1 tbsp olive oil
1 small red onion, chopped
1 small green pepper, deseeded and
  diced
1 clove garlic, chopped
1 tsp ground cumin
1 tsp smoked paprika
200g (7oz) sweet potato, peeled and
  cubed
freshly ground black pepper

1 Sift the flour, baking powder and salt into a mixing bowl. Rub the butter and white fat into the flour until it forms fine crumbs. Mix half the beaten egg with 3–4 tbsp cold water, add to the dry ingredients and mix to form a soft dough. Wrap in film and chill for 30 minutes.

2 Preheat the oven to 180°C/fan oven 160°C/Gas Mark 4. Heat the oil in a medium non-stick frying pan, add the onion and green pepper and cook for 3 minutes until soft. Add the garlic, and fry for a further minute. Add the cumin, paprika and seasoning. Fry for a further minute, stirring continuously. Add the sweet potato and toss to coat in the pan juices. Add 150ml (¼ pint) water and simmer for 15 minutes until the potato is tender. Cool.

3 Roll out the pastry on a floured work surface. Using a saucer as a template, cut out 10cm (4in) rounds. Place a tablespoon of the filling on one half of the circle, brush the edges with beaten egg, fold over, and press the edges together to seal. Brush with egg and place on a greased baking tray. Repeat with the rest of the pastry and filling. Arrange the empanadas on a baking sheet and bake for 12–15 minutes until crisp and golden. Serve warm or cold.

Busy mum's lifesaver To freeze arrange the cold cooked empanadas on a baking sheet lined with parchment and open freeze until firm. Then pack in bags or rigid containers and label. To use, cover loosely, defrost overnight and serve cold as a packed lunch; or reheat from frozen at 190°C/fan oven 170°C/Gas Mark 5 loosely covered with foil until piping hot.

Spiced carrot and coriander strudel

Think of a large spring roll but with a spiced Thai filling. It's ideal cut into slices for a packed lunch – wrap them up and send them off with a little pot of the spicy peanut sauce that goes with the Indonesian vegetable salad on page 118.

Serves 4
Prepare 20 minutes
Cook 30 minutes

2 tbsp sunflower oil
1 small onion, finely chopped
1 clove garlic, crushed
1 tsp grated fresh root ginger
½ stick lemon grass
1 red chilli, deseeded and chopped
230g (8oz) oyster mushrooms, sliced
3 medium carrots, grated
50g (2oz) bean sprouts
50g (2oz) unsalted peanuts, coarsely
   chopped
3 tbsp chopped fresh coriander
2 medium tomatoes, deseeded and
   chopped
4 tbsp sesame oil
10 large sheets filo pastry
2 tbsp soy sauce
salt and freshly ground black pepper

1 Preheat the oven to 220°C/fan oven 200°C/Gas Mark 7. Heat half the sunflower oil in a medium frying pan, add the onion and garlic and cook for 3 minutes until softened. Stir in the ginger, lemon grass and chilli and cook for a further 2 minutes. Add the mushrooms, carrots, bean sprouts, peanuts, coriander and tomatoes and mix well. Season to taste.

2 Mix 1 tablespoon of the sesame oil with the remaining sunflower oil. Lay out the filo sheets on a clean tea towel, overlapping the edges, to form a large square about 50cm (20in), trimming if necessary. Brush each sheet with the sesame and sunflower oil mixture. Cover the top two-thirds of the pastry with the filling, leaving a 2.5cm (1in) border. Sprinkle the filling with the soy sauce.

3 Roll up the strudel from the top edge, using the tea towel to help you, then transfer to a greased baking sheet, curving it to fit. Brush with the remaining sesame oil and bake for 20–25 minutes until golden and crisp. Serve hot or cold, cut into slices.

Busy mum's lifesaver Try making individual strudels. Lay a couple of sheets of filo on top of each other and brush with the oil, then fill and roll up from the short end. Cook for 15 minutes as above.

merry veggie christmas

Like most mums, I both **love and dread** the Christmas cooking marathon. I complain, of course, but wouldn't miss it for the world. However, I still worry about serving everyone **food they enjoy** Large family gatherings create all kinds of challenges for the conscientious cook who doesn't want to **dish out** the dreaded nut roast as her veggie offering. In my experience the best solution is to cook lovely meat-free dishes that complement the turkey and make **enough for everyone** That way the veggies don't feel like poor cousins. The dishes in this chapter are designed to go well with traditional **Christmas fare** so that everyone will want to try them – that's my aim for everything I cook… A lot of these dishes also make great party food. ➜

Jewelled Christmas salad

This pretty salad makes a good starter on Christmas Day as it's so quick to assemble and serve. Salted caramelised almonds are very 'on trend' at the moment and add a touch of class to the dish. Make up a batch of almonds and keep them in an airtight container to scatter on salads or serve with ice cream.

Serves 4 as a starter or 2 as a light lunch
Prepare 15 minutes

25g (1oz) whole unblanched almonds
3 tbsp granulated sugar
2 ripe pears, peeled, cored and sliced
juice of 1 lemon
100g (4oz) wild rocket
75g (3oz) Roquefort cheese, crumbled
2 tbsp extra-virgin olive oil
100g (4oz) pomegranate seeds
salt and freshly ground black pepper

1 Place the almonds in a small heavy-based frying pan with the sugar and a large pinch of salt. Heat without stirring at all and the sugar will slowly melt (if you stir the sugar, it will form into clumps and won't caramelise evenly). Keep over a medium heat until the sugar starts to caramelise – shake the pan to keep the caramel cooking evenly. When it is a rich brown colour, remove the pan from the heat and pour the almond caramel on to a lightly oiled baking sheet. Leave to cool and set, then break into pieces.

2 Toss the pear slices with half the lemon juice. Arrange the rocket on four serving plates. Scatter over the pear slices and the Roquefort.

3 Whisk together the remaining lemon juice, the olive oil and seasoning. Drizzle over the salad, scatter with pomegranate seeds and caramelised almonds and serve.

Busy mum's lifesaver You can use any blue cheese such as Stilton or even a goat's cheese instead of the Roquefort, though the latter's salty tang goes well with the sweetness of the pears.

Quail's egg, wild mushroom and spinach filo wreath

A spectacular centrepiece for the Christmas table with herb-strewn filo 'leaves'. To get ahead, make the filling and cook the eggs the day before and store them, covered, in the fridge. Then the wreath can be assembled several hours ahead on the day, refrigerated and cooked just before you need it.

Serves 6
Prepare 40 minutes
Cook 50 minutes

8 large sheets filo pastry
50g (2oz) butter, melted
fresh bay leaves, rosemary and thyme
   sprigs, to garnish

For the filling
12 quail's eggs
230g (8oz) basmati rice
350g (12oz) fresh spinach
½ tsp saffron strands
2 tbsp olive oil
2 shallots, finely chopped
50g (2oz) pine nuts, toasted
3–4 slow-roasted tomatoes or
   semi-dried tomatoes
3 tbsp chopped fresh basil
4 tbsp crème fraîche
salt and freshly ground black pepper

1 Preheat the oven to 200°C/fan oven 180°C/ Gas Mark 6. Place the quail's eggs in a pan of cold water, bring to the boil and simmer for 3 minutes. Drain and cool under cold running water, then shell.

2 Cook the rice according to the packet instructions, cool under cold running water and drain well. Blanch the spinach for a minute in boiling water, cool quickly under cold water, then drain and pat dry with kitchen paper. Soak the saffron strands in 2 tablespoons boiling water.

3 Heat the oil in a frying pan, add the shallots and cook over a medium heat for 3 minutes until softened. Remove from the heat, add the rice, saffron and its liquid, pine nuts, tomatoes, basil, crème fraîche and seasoning and stir to combine.

4 To assemble the wreath, layer three sheets of filo on top of each other, brushing each one with melted butter. Arrange half the blanched spinach leaves over the top third of the filo, leaving a 2.5cm (1in) border. Spread half the rice mixture over the spinach and place six quail's eggs along the top edge. Roll up the filo, transfer to a large greased baking sheet and shape into a semi-circle.

5 Repeat this process with three more sheets of filo and the rest of the filling ingredients. Tuck the pastry edges of the two semi-circles into each other to form a ring about 28cm (11in) in diameter.

6 Lay one of the two remaining filo sheets on top of the other, fold in half and cut out holly leaves with a metal cutter. Separate the leaves. Brush the wreath with melted butter and decorate with the leaves, then brush them with butter. Bake for 35–40 minutes until golden. Transfer to a warm serving dish and decorate with fresh herbs. Serve hot or cold.

Busy mum's lifesaver You can make individual wreaths with a single sheet of filo but I can guarantee everyone will want to try some, so it's easier to make a large one (recipe on page 126).

Celeriac and Stilton soufflés

Celeriac is a root vegetable with a strong yet subtle flavour of celery. It makes a great partner to Stilton in this soufflé. Soufflés have a reputation for being difficult to make, but if you follow the steps carefully and don't open the oven door to check while they're cooking, you shouldn't go wrong.

Serves 6–8
Prepare 20 minutes
Cook 25 minutes

a little melted butter
175g (6oz) celeriac, peeled and cubed
20g (¾oz) butter, plus extra, melted, for brushing
20g (¾oz) plain flour
75ml (3 fl oz) semi-skimmed milk
75g (3oz) Stilton cheese
3 large free-range eggs, separated
1 tsp Dijon mustard
pinch of cayenne pepper
salt and freshly ground black pepper
1 tbsp freshly grated Parmesan

1 Preheat the oven to 220°C/fan oven 200°C/Gas Mark 7. Brush 6 large ramekins or ovenproof pots with melted butter. Cook the celeriac in a pan of boiling water for 10–12 minutes until tender. Drain well, then purée in a vegetable mouli or a food processor.

2 Meanwhile, melt the butter in a small saucepan over a medium heat. Stir in the flour and cook, stirring, for 1 minute. Off the heat, gradually whisk in the milk, then return the pan to the heat, Bring to the boil, stirring, to give a thick, smooth sauce.

3 Remove the pan from the heat and stir in the celeriac purée and crumble in the Stilton, followed by the egg yolks, mustard, cayenne and seasoning. Beat together well.

4 Whisk the egg whites in a clean, dry bowl until stiff but not dry, then carefully fold them into the cheese and celeriac base. Spoon the soufflé mixture into the prepared dishes and sprinkle with the Parmesan. Place on a baking sheet and bake for 10–12 minutes until well risen and golden. Serve immediately.

Busy mum's lifesaver To get ahead, make up the soufflé base and have the egg whites ready to whisk. Then all you need to do is warm the celeriac base very gently and fold in the whites. You can also freeze the uncooked soufflés in their dishes and then cook them directly from frozen for 15–20 minutes. They will rise up but not quite as much. This mixture will also make 1 large soufflé, which you'll need to cook for 18–20 minutes depending on the diameter of the dish. Always remember to season any egg dish thoroughly to bring out the full flavour.

Parsnip and walnut roulade

A bit of a cliché but one that works. Organic or home-grown parsnips have a more intense flavour and will make a real difference to this dish. It tastes great hot or cold and is popular with my family as part of a Boxing Day spread. Cut it into thick slices before you serve it, so that people can help themselves.

Serves 4
Prepare 20 minutes
Cook 15 minutes

350g (12oz) parsnips, peeled
   and sliced
15g (½oz) butter
1 tbsp plain flour
4 large free-range eggs, separated
25g (1oz) walnut pieces, toasted and
   finely chopped
large pinch of cayenne pepper
3 tbsp freshly grated Parmesan
salt and freshly ground black pepper

For the filling
25g (1oz) butter
1 medium onion, sliced
1 tbsp plain flour
150ml (¼ pint) semi-skimmed milk
75g (3oz) strong Cheddar, grated
1 small bunch watercress, leaves
   finely chopped

1 Preheat the oven to 190°C/fan oven 170°C/ Gas Mark 5. Cook the parsnips in boiling water for about 15 minutes until tender, then drain thoroughly. Purée in a blender or food processor.

2 Melt the butter in a medium pan, stir in the flour and cook for 1 minute. Beat in the parsnip purée and the egg yolks, then remove from the heat and season well. Stir in the walnuts and cayenne. Whisk the egg whites until stiff and carefully fold them into the parsnip mixture.

3 Pour the mixture into a greased and lined 20 x 30cm (8 x 12in) Swiss roll tin, smooth the surface and scatter the Parmesan over the top. Bake for 15 minutes until golden and firm to the touch.

4 While the roulade is cooking, make the filling. Melt the butter in a medium pan and cook the onion over a low heat for 10 minutes until soft and golden. Stir in the flour and cook for 1 minute. Remove from the heat and gradually whisk in the milk, then return to the heat and bring to the boil, stirring constantly, until the sauce is thick and smooth. Remove from the heat again and stir in the Cheddar, watercress and seasoning to taste.

5 Turn the hot roulade out on to a sheet of baking parchment, peel off the lining paper and spread the roulade with the filling. Roll it up carefully from a short end, using the baking parchment to help you. Transfer to a warm serving dish and serve immediately.

Busy mum's lifesaver Use any strong cheese for the filling – it's a good way of using up leftovers from the Christmas cheeseboard for a Boxing Day lunch. If you're short of time make a filling with soured cream, crumbled Stilton and chopped watercress but ideally only do this if you're serving the roulade cold.

Caramelised cabbage and goat's cheese croustade

This glorious indulgent pie uses quick homemade flaky pastry (which is also good for mince pies), but do use readymade puff pastry made with butter if short of time. I rarely have the time or the inclination to make pastry these days but, when I do, it's always for a dish that will really benefit from the superior flavour and texture. This croustade is well worth the effort.

Serves 4–6
Prepare 30 minutes
Cook 45 minutes

½ small Savoy cabbage, finely
   shredded
25g (1oz) butter
1 tsp caster sugar
½ tsp ground cumin
1 medium onion, sliced
100g (4oz) goat's cheese, crumbled
3 tbsp freshly grated Parmesan
4 tbsp double cream
salt and freshly ground black
   pepper
beaten egg, to glaze

For the pastry
175g (6oz) butter
230g (8oz) plain flour
pinch of salt

1 To make the pastry, place the block of butter in the freezer until hard. Sift the flour and salt into a bowl. Remove the butter from the freezer, wrap one end in foil and coarsely grate it into the flour. Stir it in with the blade of a knife just until each piece is coated with flour. Sprinkle with 3–4 tablespoons iced water and mix to a soft dough with a round-bladed knife. Finally bring it together with your hands to form a firm ball, then wrap and chill for 30 minutes.

2 Preheat the oven to 220°C/fan oven 200°C/Gas Mark 7. Cook the cabbage in boiling water for a couple of minutes until wilted, then drain thoroughly. Melt half the butter in a frying pan and add the cabbage and sugar. Cook over a low heat for 5–6 minutes until tender. Stir in the cumin and seasoning. In a separate pan, cook the onion in the remaining butter over a medium heat for 10 minutes until golden.

3 Roll out half the pastry on a lightly floured work surface and cut out a 23cm (9in) circle, using a plate as a guide. Put the pastry circle on a baking sheet and brush the edges with water. Spoon the cabbage mixture over the centre, leaving a 2.5cm (1in) border, then top with the onion. Crumble the goat's cheese over the top, sprinkle with the Parmesan and spoon over the cream. Season well.

4 Roll out the remaining pastry to a circle just larger than the base and use to cover the filling. Pinch the edges well to seal and mark with a fork around the edge. Mark a lattice pattern on the top with a knife, brush with beaten egg and bake for 20–25 minutes until the pastry is puffy and golden. Transfer to a warm serving plate and cut into wedges.

Busy mum's lifesaver This freezes well so I make up a couple and keep them in the freezer for emergencies. Cook from frozen loosely covered with foil for 45–50 minutes at the same temperature, removing the foil for the last 15 minutes for the pastry to brown.

Chestnut and cranberry casserole with port

I just have to hear the song 'Chestnuts Roasting on an Open Fire' and I think of this dish! It's a really warming way to feed friends and family over the holiday period. Make it a day or two ahead – or even further in advance and freeze it – as the flavours will develop with keeping.

➡ Serve with buttery baked potatoes or wholegrain rice.

Serves 4–6
Prepare 15 minutes
Cook 1 hour

3 tbsp olive oil
350g (12oz) shallots or button onions, peeled
350g (12oz) Chantenay carrots, trimmed
1 medium celeriac, peeled and cubed
2 cloves garlic, chopped
650g (1¼lb) peeled chestnuts, vacuum-packed or frozen
1 tbsp plain flour
grated rind and juice of 1 orange
3 tbsp chopped fresh flat-leaf parsley
1 tbsp chopped fresh rosemary
1 bay leaf
½ tsp ground mace
½ tsp ground cloves
300ml (½ pint) red wine
150ml (¼ pint) vegetable stock
230g (8oz) fresh cranberries
4 tbsp port
salt and freshly ground black pepper
chopped fresh parsley and finely shredded orange rind, to garnish

1 Heat the oil in a flameproof casserole and cook the shallots or button onions over a medium heat for 5–6 minutes until golden. Remove from the pan with a slotted spoon. Add the carrots, celeriac, garlic and chestnuts to the pan and cook, stirring, for about 6–8 minutes until golden.

2 Return the shallots to the pan with the flour and cook for 1 minute. Stir in the orange rind and juice, parsley, rosemary, bay leaf, spices and seasoning, then pour in the wine and stock. Bring to the boil, then cover and simmer for a further 20 minutes.

3 Stir in the cranberries and port and simmer for a further 20 minutes until the sauce is reduced and the chestnuts are tender. Garnish with chopped parsley and shredded orange rind and serve.

Busy mum's lifesaver Make this dish ahead as it improves with keeping. When cooking for a mixed group, double the quantities and fry off 675g (1½lb) cubed stewing steak or cubed venison to add to half of the mixture after frying the shallots. Add an extra 300ml (½ pint) stock and cook the meat casserole for an extra 1½ hours until the meat is tender. Finish as above.

Fresh chestnuts have a wonderful flavour and texture but peeling them is hard work. However, if you put them in the microwave for a few minutes it loosens the skins. Simply pierce the chestnuts with a sharp knife, then cook them four at a time on high for 1 minute until the skins split. It works a dream and they peel easily.

Spiced pumpkin and sweet potato gratin

This tasty dish goes perfectly with a classic Christmas turkey meal – all the non-veggies love it too and the flavours of ginger and sage are festive and warming. A large dish served with a salad also makes a great Christmas Eve supper for when everyone gets in from carol services – or after a day Christmas shopping – as you can leave it sitting happily in a low oven.

→ Serve with bread and a green salad.

Serves 4–6
Prepare 15 minutes
Cook 1 hour

500g (1lb 2oz) pumpkin, peeled,
   deseeded and cubed
500g (1lb 2oz) sweet potatoes, peeled
   and cubed
2 cloves garlic, roughly chopped
2 tbsp chopped fresh sage
1 tsp ground ginger
1 tsp ground cumin
150ml (¼ pint) vegetable stock or
   white wine
150ml (¼ pint) single cream
25g (1oz) seed mix
25g (1oz) white breadcrumbs
50g (2oz) hard goat's cheese, grated
salt and freshly ground black pepper

1 Preheat the oven to 180°C/fan oven 160°C/Gas Mark 4. Place the pumpkin and sweet potatoes in a shallow 2 litre (3½ pint) ovenproof dish or roasting tin. Scatter over the garlic, sage, ginger, cumin and seasoning. Pour over the stock or wine, cover loosely with foil and bake in the oven for 40–45 minutes until the squash is almost tender.

2 Increase the oven temperature to 200°C/fan oven 180°C/Gas Mark 6. Pour the cream over the vegetables and scatter with the seed mix, breadcrumbs and goat's cheese. Return to the oven for a further 12–15 minutes until the top is bubbling and golden.

Pappardelle with mushrooms, chestnuts and cranberry

This is one of the dishes I bring out when I want to convince meat eaters that veggie food can have such intense, satisfying flavours you won't miss meat at all. It's a favourite Christmas Eve supper in our household and everyone at the photography session was convinced by the smell alone. The finished dish just proved the point.

Serves 3–4
Prepare 10 minutes
Cook 20 minutes

2 tbsp olive oil
1 small onion, finely chopped
1 medium carrot, diced
2 sticks celery, diced
100g (4oz) small chestnut mushrooms, halved
150ml (¼ pint) vegetable stock
150ml (¼ pint) red wine
1 tbsp chopped fresh thyme
200g (7oz) vacuum-packed whole chestnuts
1 tbsp sun-dried tomato paste
2 tbsp cranberry sauce
250g (9oz) pappardelle pasta
salt and freshly ground black pepper
freshly grated Parmesan, to serve

1 Heat the oil in a large sauté pan and fry the onion, carrot and celery together for 3–4 minutes until softened but not browned. Add the mushrooms and brown quickly over a high heat for a minute or two.

2 Stir in the stock, wine, thyme, chestnuts, tomato paste, cranberry sauce and seasoning and simmer, covered, for 15 minutes until the liquid has reduced. Cook the pappardelle for 2–3 minutes or according to pack instructions, in a large pan of boiling water until just tender. Drain the pasta and toss with the sauce. Serve with grated Parmesan.

Busy mum's lifesaver To serve both meat eaters and veggies, divide the softened vegetable mix in half and add mushrooms to one half, sliced sausages to the other and then follow step 2, dividing the ingredients between two pans.

Spiced root vegetable ragout with couscous

A good spicy veg stew is always a hit in cold weather and winter root veg soak up the spicy flavours beautifully. You'll really notice the difference in flavour when you use home-grown veg or buy from the farmers' market. The tastes are far more intense and the textures are better too.

→ Serve with broccoli or Savoy cabbage.

Serves 4
Prepare 10 minutes
Cook 25 minutes

200g (7oz) couscous
1 tbsp olive oil
50g (2oz) mixed seeds
large pinch of ground cloves (optional)
   or large pinch of mixed spice

For the ragout
2 tbsp olive oil
1 large red onion, sliced
2 cloves garlic, finely chopped
1 tsp each smoked paprika, ground
   ginger and cinnamon
230g (8oz) each baby carrots and
   turnips, scrubbed, topped and
   tailed
1 medium swede, peeled and cubed
2–3 parsnips, peeled and sliced
300ml (½ pint) vegetable stock
1 tsp tomato purée
100g (4oz) green beans, trimmed
   and halved
400g can chickpeas, drained
1–2 tsp harissa
salt and freshly ground black pepper
2 tbsp chopped fresh coriander,
   to serve

1 Heat the oil in a large flameproof casserole and add the onion and garlic. Cook gently, stirring, for 3 minutes until softened, then add the spices and cook for another minute. Add the root vegetables, stock, tomato purée and seasoning and simmer for 10–15 minutes until the vegetables are tender. Stir in the beans and chickpeas and simmer for a further 5 minutes.

2 Meanwhile, place the couscous in a bowl and pour over 200ml (7fl oz) boiling water. Leave to stand for 10 minutes then stir with a fork to break up any lumps. Heat the oil for the couscous in a large frying pan and add the couscous, seeds, spice and seasoning. Heat through gently then spoon into a large heated serving dish.

3 Stir the harissa into the ragout and spoon over the couscous. Scatter with chopped coriander and serve.

Busy mum's lifesaver Use the spice mix ras el hanout instead of the individual spices. Vary the veg with the season – add courgettes, broccoli, cauliflower, sweet potato or what you have to hand. I sometimes add chopped soft apricots or dates.

My Christmas pudding

Neither too dark nor too light, with just the right moisture content: this recipe has slowly evolved over the 20-odd years I've been making Christmas puddings and I think I'm finally there with the definitive veggie version. Butter works well here; not only is it suitable for vegetarians, unlike traditional suet, but it also gives the pudding a lovely flavour and texture.

→ Serve with cream, custard or the spiced rum and orange butter on page 142.

Serves 8
Prepare 30 minutes
Cook 8 hours

150g (5oz) raisins
150g (5oz) sultanas
75g (3oz) currants
300ml (½ pint) Guinness or brown ale
50g (2oz) candied peel, chopped
50g (2oz) pine nuts, chopped
50g (2oz) blanched almonds, chopped
1 eating apple, grated
75g (3oz) carrot, grated
100g (4oz) self-raising flour
2 tsp mixed spice
1 tsp freshly grated nutmeg
100g (4oz) butter
100g (4oz) dark muscovado sugar
2 large free-range eggs
100g (4oz) fresh breadcrumbs
grated rind and juice of 1 lemon
3–4 tbsp brandy or milk

1 Place the raisins, sultanas and currants in a large mixing bowl, pour over the Guinness and leave overnight to soak, covered with a clean tea towel.

2 The next day, stir in the candied peel, pine nuts, almonds, apple and carrot into the soaked fruit. In a separate bowl, sift the flour with the spices. Beat the butter with the sugar until fluffy, then beat in the eggs one at a time. Fold in the flour and then stir in the fruit mixture with the breadcrumbs, lemon rind and juice and brandy or milk. Mix thoroughly, then spoon into a greased 1.75 litre (3 pint) pudding basin.

3 Cover the pudding with greaseproof paper and foil, pleated in the centre, and tie securely with string. Steam for 5 hours, topping up the pan regularly with boiling water. Remove the pudding from the pan and leave to cool. Re-cover the pudding with fresh greaseproof paper and foil and store in a cool dark place for at least a month. You can pour over a little brandy once or twice during storage to help the pud mature!

4 On the day, steam the pudding for a further 3 hours, turn out on to a warm serving plate and top with a sprig of holly.

Mincemeat and cranberry star mince pies

Classic mince pies can be overly sweet – adding cranberries cuts though the sweetness. Make sure you buy vegetarian mincemeat, not one made with beef suet. The almond frangipane topping is also a family favourite. Children can have lots of fun getting icing sugar everywhere dusting the star shapes on to the finished mince pies.

→ Serve with thick cream or the spiced rum and orange butter on page 142.

Makes 24
Prepare 20 minutes
Cook 15 minutes

350g pack readymade shortcrust
   pastry made with butter
230g (8oz) vegetarian mincemeat
100g (4oz) fresh cranberries
100g (4oz) butter
100g (4oz) caster sugar
2 large free-range eggs
100g (4oz) ground almonds
50g (2oz) flaked almonds

1 Preheat the oven to 190°C/fan oven 170°C/Gas Mark 5. Roll out the pastry on a lightly floured surface and cut out 7.5cm (3in) circles and use to line 24 pie tins. Mix together the mincemeat and cranberries and put a spoonful in each case.

2 Cream the butter and sugar together till pale and beat in the eggs one at a time. Fold in the ground almonds and spread over the mincemeat. Sprinkle with the flaked almonds.

3 Bake for 12–15 minutes until golden. Cool on a wire rack. Dust the mince pies with icing sugar, using stencils to make star patterns (see below). Serve them warm or cold.

Busy mum's lifesaver To make the stencils, cut a circle of card the same diameter as the pies and cut a star from the centre of the circle. Dust half the pies with icing sugar using the cardboard star and the other half using the circle stencil.

Spiced rum and orange butter

You can buy really delicious spiced rum now – I cook with it on a regular basis. It's perfect here and adds a little twist to traditional rum butter. If you can't find it, use regular rum and add a large pinch of mixed spice instead – it won't be quite the same but it's along the right lines. Try adding spiced rum to baked bananas, cocktails or a Christmas trifle or chocolate mousse!

→ Serve with the mince pies on page 140.

Serves 8
Prepare 10 minutes
Chill 2–3 hours

175g (6oz) butter
175g (6oz) light muscovado sugar
4–5 tbsp spiced rum
grated rind of 1 orange

1 Cream the butter until soft then add the sugar and beat until pale and fluffy. Gradually beat in the rum and orange rind. Pile into a bowl and chill for several hours.

Busy mum's lifesaver The rum butter will keep in the fridge for up to a week in a covered container.

going solo

You may have got the message by now that I am not a fan of cooking separate dishes for different members of the family at one sitting. Having said that, we all eat on our own every now and then – mums once the kids are in bed, teenagers on the way out to some social or school commitment, or dads back from the football. So this chapter has recipes designed for when you're eating alone – they're not meant to be served as little veggie islands in the midst of a meat feast! These are also useful dishes to teach children (or partners) to cook for themselves. ⟶

Baked mushrooms with goat's cheese

If I'm cooking something special just for myself the dish must need practically no preparation and the ingredients should already be in the fridge. One particular night all I had were flat mushrooms and goat's cheese, which led to this recipe. I was so impressed that I promptly cooked it for friends the following night as a starter.

→ Serve with walnut bread and thin green beans.

Serves 1
Prepare 5 minutes
Cook 15 minutes

2 large flat mushrooms, wiped and
    stalks removed
2 tsp black olive paste
50g (2oz) goat's cheese, sliced
1 tsp pine nuts
1 tbsp olive oil
salt and freshly ground black pepper
2–3 fresh basil leaves, shredded

1 Preheat the oven to 200°C/fan oven 180°C/Gas Mark 6. Spread the inside of the mushroom caps with olive paste. Place them in a shallow gratin dish or small roasting tin.

2 Arrange a slice of goat's cheese on each mushroom, scatter with pine nuts and drizzle with oil and season.

3 Bake the mushrooms for 15 minutes until the cheese is melted and golden and the mushrooms are tender. Scatter over the basil and serve immediately.

Busy mum's lifesaver Pick a rinded goat's cheese with a diameter similar to that of the mushrooms for this quick dish. The sliced cheese should sit neatly within each mushroom's cap. Try pesto instead of black olive paste.

Piperade

Basically this is Provençal-style scrambled eggs and totally delicious. I know veggies can get fed up with endless omelette variations but the humble egg really is my fall-back favourite, especially as I keep my own hens. Piperade is a great meal for anyone in a hurry.

→ Serve with sliced baguette and a green salad.

Serves 1
Prepare 10 minutes
Cook 15 minutes

1 tbsp olive oil
½ small red onion, thinly sliced
1 clove garlic, finely chopped
½ red Romano pepper, deseeded and thinly sliced
½ yellow pepper, deseeded and thinly sliced
½ red chilli, deseeded and chopped
1 vine tomato, quartered and chopped
2 medium free-range eggs, beaten
salt and freshly ground black pepper
chopped flat leaf parsley, to garnish

1 Heat half the oil in a small frying pan and add the onion, garlic, peppers and chilli and cook for 8–10 minutes on a low heat till soft and golden. Stir in the tomato and seasoning and cook over a high heat for 3–4 minutes until any moisture is evaporated. Remove and keep warm.

2 Heat the remaining oil in the pan and add the eggs and seasoning. Stir over a low heat until curds form, continue stirring till soft and creamy and not quite set. Stir in the pepper mixture, scatter with chopped parsley and serve.

Busy mum's lifesaver For non-veggies add cubed chorizo when you add the chopped tomatoes.

Baby leaf and edamame salad with garlic croûtons

A staple of Japanese cooking, edamame beans are baby soya beans and they are now grown here in the UK – look out for them in supermarkets. Use them wherever you'd use broad beans, in recipes like this lovely spring salad, for example.

Serves 1
Prepare 10 minutes
Cook 5 minutes

1 tbsp olive oil
1 small slice sourdough bread, cut
   into cubes
½ clove garlic, crushed
100g (4oz) podded edamame beans
75g (3oz) baby salad leaves
3 spring onions, sliced
50g (4oz) feta cheese, crumbled
1 tbsp chopped fresh mint
1 tsp white wine vinegar
1 tbsp extra-virgin oil
salt and freshly ground black pepper

1 To make the croutons, heat the oil in a small non-stick frying pan over a medium heat. Add the bread cubes and garlic and fry until golden. Remove the croûtons from the pan with a slotted spoon and drain well on kitchen paper. Sprinkle with a little salt.

2 Cook the beans in a small pan of boiling water for 2 minutes until just tender. Drain, refresh under cold water and drain again. Pat dry with kitchen paper.

3 Place the beans in a salad bowl with the salad leaves, spring onions and feta cheese. Whisk together the mint, vinegar, oil and seasoning. Add the croûtons to the salad with the dressing, toss gently to coat the leaves and serve immediately.

Busy mum's lifesaver If you only have frozen broad beans, blanch them then slip off the grey skins before adding to the salad – it makes all the difference. This is a good recipe to make if you grow your own salad.

Mushroom and coconut curry

There is a wonderful veggie restaurant in Edinburgh where they always made a great mushroom curry – which inspired this dish. It's quick and easy for one but try doubling it up and keeping half, as it improves in flavour in the fridge.

⟶ Serve with steamed brown rice.

Serves 1
Prepare 5 minutes
Cook 20 minutes

1 tbsp vegetable oil
½ small onion, finely chopped
1 clove garlic, finely chopped
1 tsp chopped fresh root ginger
½ tsp each ground cumin and coriander
large pinch each of turmeric and cayenne pepper
230g (8oz) chestnut mushrooms, halved
75ml (3fl oz) coconut milk
½ tsp garam masala
1 tbsp lemon juice
salt and freshly ground black pepper
chopped fresh coriander, to garnish

1 Heat half the oil in a small pan and add the onion, garlic and ginger and cook for 5 minutes on a low heat till soft. Stir in the spices and cook over a high heat for a minute then add the mushrooms and cook over a medium heat for 8–10 minutes until the mushrooms are tender.

2 Add the coconut milk, garam masala and seasoning and simmer for 5 minutes. Stir in the lemon juice, scatter with chopped coriander and serve.

Grilled aubergine bruschetta with tomato salsa

Bruschetta is an easy summer snack or lunch. The better the bread, the finer the finished dish – I keep ciabatta rolls in the freezer to make this quickly for whoever needs feeding in a hurry (or they can make it themselves!). It's also good with sourdough and is a thrifty way of using up stale bread.

Serves 1
Prepare 10 minutes
Cook 10 minutes

1 small aubergine, about 175g (6oz), trimmed
1 tbsp olive oil
½ clove garlic, chopped
1 tbsp chopped fresh mint
salt and freshly ground black pepper
a ciabatta roll (ideally with olives), halved

For the tomato salsa
½ green chilli, deseeded and chopped
1 plum tomato, halved
1 spring onion, sliced

1 Preheat the grill to high. Cut the aubergine lengthways into slices about 1cm (¼in) thick and arrange them on the grill pan. Mix together the oil, garlic, mint and seasoning and brush the aubergine slices with half the mixture. Grill for about 5 minutes until golden, then turn the slices over, brush with oil and grill until golden.

2 Make the tomato salsa. Put the chilli, tomato, spring onion and seasoning in a small blender or food processor and process lightly until chopped; the salsa should be quite coarse, not a purée.

3 Toast the roll on both sides under the grill. Drizzle with any remaining oil then top with the grilled aubergine and spoon on the salsa.

Busy mum's lifesaver Try adding a grilled pepper, seeded and cut into strips, to the topping. Use pesto instead of the salsa if in a hurry.

Tricolore focaccia sandwich

The classic Italian salad of avocado, tomato and mozzarella is known as tricolore after the Italian flag. In a bun it's great student snack food or a busy mum's lunch. As ever, the better the ingredients, the finer the dish: that's buffalo mozzarella, properly ripe tomatoes and really good pesto and oil.

Serves 1
Prepare 5 minutes
Cook 3 minutes

1 focaccia roll (ideally with rosemary and salt)
1 tbsp pesto sauce
1 ripe tomato, sliced
50g (2oz) mozzarella, sliced
½ ripe avocado, sliced
1 tsp extra-virgin olive oil
salt and freshly ground black pepper

1 Preheat the oven to 200°C/fan oven 180°C/Gas Mark 6. Split the roll in half horizontally and toast it on both sides. Spread the bottom half with the pesto sauce and arrange the tomato and mozzarella on top. Top with the avocado and season.

2 Drizzle the oil over the cut side of the other half of the roll and place it on top of the avocado. Put it in the oven for 3–4 minutes until the cheese just starts to melt. Serve immediately.

Busy mum's lifesaver It's not worth heating the oven just for this roll as it tastes fine served cold but if you've got the oven going (or if you have an Aga), a bit of heat does encourage the flavours to meld together.

Spring onion and chickpea omelette

An indifferently prepared omelette used to be the fate of many a vegetarian when eating out. It's one of those dishes that has to be just right for the person who's going to eat it: some people (like me) prefer an omelette that's running in the centre, others like a firm set. A good omelette should combine the two, with a golden exterior concealing a moist flavoursome inside. It's well worth re-discovering the joys of a properly cooked version in the comfort of your own home.

➡ Serve with a tomato and red onion salad.

Serves 1
Prepare 5 minutes
Cook 5 minutes

1 tsp olive oil
4 spring onions, chopped
½ garlic clove, crushed
75g (3oz) canned chickpeas, drained and rinsed
3 medium free-range eggs
pinch of turmeric
1 cherry tomato, deseeded and chopped
1 tbsp chopped fresh flat-leaf parsley
small knob of butter
salt and freshly ground black pepper

1 Heat half the oil in a small frying pan over a medium heat. Add the spring onions, garlic and chickpeas and cook for 3 minutes, stirring occasionally, until the spring onions are wilted. Remove from the pan and keep warm.

2 Beat the eggs in a bowl with the turmeric, tomato, parsley and seasoning. Heat the butter in the cleaned pan over a medium heat. When it is foaming, add the egg mixture and cook, stirring gently with a fork to bring the uncooked egg to the centre, until the base begins to set. Stop stirring and continue cooking for a minute or two until the base is golden – the centre of the omelette should still be a little runny.

3 Spoon the chickpea mixture on to one half of the omelette, fold over, slide on to a warm plate and serve.

Spinach and ricotta tortelloni with broad beans, lemon and sage

You can buy such good filled pasta shapes now: I keep a pack in the freezer permanently as they make great quick meals for hungry young (or not so young). This is really easy and so delicious I make it practically daily when the broad beans in my veg garden are ready. Pumpkin-filled pasta also works well.

Serves 1
Prepare 5 minutes
Cook 5 minutes

small knob of butter
15g (½oz) pine nuts
1 tsp grated lemon rind
4 fresh sage leaves
2 tbsp single cream
200g (7oz) fresh broad beans,
    podded or 75g (3oz) frozen
    broad beans
150g (5oz) spinach and ricotta
    tortelloni
salt and freshly ground black pepper
freshly grated Parmesan, to serve

1 Heat the butter in a small pan. Add the pine nuts and cook for a minute. Add the lemon rind and sage and heat for a further minute. Add the cream and seasoning and heat through. Keep warm.

2 Bring a pan of water to the boil, add the broad beans and cook for a minute then add the pasta and cook for 3 minutes until tender. Drain and toss with the sauce. Serve with freshly grated Parmesan.

Roasted tomatoes with chickpeas

This salad is an ideal quick supper or lunch for one, but can easily be scaled up to feed a crowd. It's a version of a dish I ate in Sicily when I spent a week there at a fantastic cookery school, where I learnt the importance of superb ingredients, to keep things simple – and also that it does a mother a lot of good to go away on her own once in a while. The salad was served with barbecued squid and seafood couscous but it was so good I could have eaten it on its own.

➡ Serve with bread to mop up the juices and a green salad.

Serves 1
Prepare 5 minutes
Cook 20 minutes

3 cloves garlic
3 ripe plum tomatoes
½ x 400g can chickpeas, drained
1 small red onion, sliced
2 tbsp chopped fresh basil
1 tbsp extra-virgin olive oil
salt and freshly ground black pepper

1 Preheat the oven to 200°C/fan oven 180°C/Gas Mark 6. Place the garlic and tomatoes in a small roasting tin and cook in the oven for 15–20 minutes until the flesh is soft.

2 Place the chickpeas in a salad bowl with the onion, basil, oil and seasoning.

3 Skin the tomatoes and garlic cloves and roughly chop the flesh. Add to the salad and mix well, and leave to stand for 10–15 minutes for the flavours to develop.

Busy mum's lifesaver I always say life is too short to skin a tomato, but here it does make a difference and for one person is (almost) worth the effort. But if you're in a hurry, don't bother.

pud paradise

You may ask yourself what puddings are doing in a veggie book, as they tend on the whole to be meat free and there are plenty of recipes out there already. My answer is that I have a very sweet tooth and love making them. On a more serious note, these puddings are also a good way to get the whole family to eat more fruit, and they're so much better for children than lots of processed puddings, which may be high in sugar, salt and other things we want to avoid. ➜

Rose-petal raspberry meringues

This is a tribute to those 1970s parties where there were always towers of little pairs of meringues sandwiched with cream – so simple but everyone loved them. In this recipe rose petals infuse the caster sugar with their delicate perfume (you can also use the sugar for sponges, shortbread and cupcakes). Substitute any summer fruit in season.

Serves 6–8
Prepare 20 minutes
Cook 2 hours

3 egg whites
175g (6oz) rose-petal sugar (see below)
100g (4oz) fresh raspberries
2 tbsp caster sugar
150ml (¼ pint) double cream, lightly whipped
rose petals and extra raspberries, to decorate
icing sugar, for dusting

1 Preheat the oven to 140°C/fan oven 120°C/Gas Mark 1. Place the egg whites in a really clean bowl and whisk until stiff enough to form peaks. Whisk in the rose sugar, a tablespoon at a time, until the mixture is really thick and glossy. Pile in small spoonfuls on to baking sheets lined with baking parchment. Bake for 1½–2 hours until very pale golden and crisp, then turn off the oven and leave to cool overnight. Once cold, store the meringues in an airtight container until needed.

2 To assemble, roughly mash the raspberries and caster sugar with a fork, then fold into the whipped cream. Use the cream to sandwich the meringues in pairs. Pile on to a serving plate and scatter with rose petals and extra raspberries. Dust with icing sugar.

Busy mum's lifesaver Make the flower sugar up to a week before you want to use it. Pick rose petals (or any flower heads, such as lavender or marigolds) that haven't been sprayed with chemicals – you need about 10–12 tbsp of roughly chopped petals. Process or blend the petals with 300g (10oz) golden caster sugar until broken into tiny pieces. Tip into an airtight jar and seal. Store in a cool dark place for a week. You can sieve the flower pieces out: I like to leave them in for colour and texture but it's up to you whether you mind spitting out tiny pieces of flowers!

Brown sugar plums with soured cream

This is a Gwynn family classic – it's an easy way to create a lovely pudding at the last minute.
You can use any stone fruit but it's also good for using up bananas that are just about to go over.

➡ Serve hot or cold with the ginger crunchies on page 190 or the biscotti on page 184.

Serves 4
Prepare 5 minutes
Cook 25 minutes

8 fresh plums, halved and stoned
2 tbsp light muscovado sugar
½ tsp ground cinnamon
300ml (½ pint) soured cream
3 tbsp demerara sugar

1 Heat the oven to 220°C/fan oven 200°C/ Gas Mark 7. Arrange the plums in the base of a gratin dish or roasting tin, cut-side up, to make a tight-fitting single layer. Mix together the muscovado sugar and cinnamon and sprinkle over the plums. Bake for 20–25 minutes until tender and the juices are running.

2 Spoon the soured cream over the top and sprinkle with the demerara sugar. If you want to, place the dish under a hot grill until the sugar melts but it's not essential.

Chocolate raspberry terrine

This is a real show-stopper of a pud – a combination of chocolate mousse, alcohol-soaked cake and raspberries is always a sure-fire winner. Don't make it look too perfect, though, as I think slightly homemade looks more appealing. The terrine is ideal for parties as it's best made a day ahead to allow the flavours to combine, but don't turn it out and decorate it until a couple of hours before you need it.

Serves 6–8
Prepare 40 minutes
Cook 30 minutes

2 large free-range eggs
50g (2oz) caster sugar
few drops of vanilla essence
40g (1½ oz) plain flour
1 tbsp cocoa powder
25g (1oz) butter, melted and cooled
2 tbsp brandy
1 tsp instant coffee granules dissolved in 75ml (3fl oz) boiling water
400g (14oz) fresh raspberries
cocoa powder, chocolate curls and extra raspberries, to decorate

For the chocolate mousse
175g (6oz) good-quality dark chocolate
300ml (½ pint) double cream

1 Make the chocolate sponge first. Preheat the oven to 190°C/fan oven 170°C/Gas Mark 5. Place the eggs, sugar and vanilla essence in a mixing bowl and whisk with an electric mixer until very thick and pale – the mixture should hold its shape on the surface if you drop a spoonful on to it. Sift the flour and cocoa powder over the surface and fold in quickly and lightly, then fold in the melted butter. Pour into a greased and base-lined 10 x 30 x 7.5cm (4 x 12 x 3in) loaf tin – it will only just half fill it – and bake for 25–30 minutes until well risen and firm to the touch. Turn out on to a wire rack to cool.

2 To make the mousse, break up the chocolate and place in a small bowl set over a pan of simmering water. Stir until melted, then cool slightly. Whip the cream until floppy then whisk in half the cooled chocolate. Fold in the remaining chocolate with a metal spoon.

3 To assemble the terrine, cut the cake in half horizontally and place one half back in the loaf tin. Mix the brandy and coffee together and sprinkle half over the cake in the tin. Spread half the raspberries over the cake and top with chocolate mousse. Level the surface, top with the remaining raspberries and arrange the other half of the cake on top. Sprinkle with the rest of the brandy and coffee.

4 Cover the terrine with foil, arrange weights along the foil (cans of beans are ideal) and chill for several hours. To serve, run a knife that has been dipped in hot water around the edges of the terrine, then carefully turn it out on to a serving plate. Dust with cocoa powder and arrange chocolate curls and raspberries on top. When ready to serve, cut the layered terrine with a warm knife.

Busy mum's lifesaver Make sure the terrine is really chilled to make it easier to turn out. If it collapses a bit, hide any cracks with the cocoa and chocolate curls. You could even use a bought chocolate sponge loaf and just cut pieces to fit. Make chocolate curls using a swivel-edged vegetable peeler and a thick bar of dark chocolate.

Marinated summer fruit with vanilla ice cream

Summer berries soaked in booze – a marvellous way to finish a summer supper outside in the garden. The recipe uses fortified wines so don't serve the pud to small children or drivers – you have been warned. I keep a bottle of Pedro Jimenez sherry specially for this dish and to pour over ice cream: it's supremely dark, rich and fragrant, and expensive – but a little goes a long way.

➡ Serve with good-quality vanilla ice cream and the biscotti on page 184.

Serves 4
Prepare 5 minutes, plus 2–3 hours marinating

650g (1¼lb) mixed summer berries: strawberries, raspberries, blueberries and cherries
50g (2oz) caster sugar
6–8 tbsp Pedro Jimenez sherry or Vin Santo

1 Wash and prepare the fruit. Halve the strawberries if large and stone the cherries if using. Place in a large bowl and sprinkle with the sugar. Pour over the sherry, cover and leave to marinate in the fridge for 2–3 hours.

2 To serve, spoon the fruit into glass dishes and top with a scoop of ice cream. Drizzle some of the fruit and sherry juices over the ice cream and serve with the biscotti.

Red fruit flambée

At its best, fresh soft summer fruit needs little enhancement, but when it's past its peak, this quick pud uses it to advantage. If you are worried about setting fire to the kitchen or singeing your eyebrows, omit the flambéing and simmer the fruit for one minute after adding the brandy, to get rid of the alcohol.
➡ Serve with vanilla ice cream or thick double cream.

Serves 4
Prepare 5 minutes
Cook 10 minutes

2 oranges
230g (8oz) fresh strawberries, halved
4 plums, halved and stoned
75g (3oz) redcurrants, removed
   from their strings
230g (8oz) fresh raspberries
75–100g (3–4oz) golden granulated
   sugar
4 tablespoons brandy or rum

1 Grate the rind from one of the oranges then squeeze the juice from both. Put the rind, strawberries, plums, redcurrants and raspberries together in a bowl and mix thoroughly.

2 Put the sugar in a heavy-based shallow pan or frying pan over a high heat and heat until it melts and starts to caramelise and go golden brown. Don't stir it: if you do, it will form into sticky lumps as it melts. Just move the pan around on the heat to get the heat to the right areas. This will take about 3 minutes. Stir the orange juice into the caramel – watch out as the sugar will splutter – then lower the heat and continue stirring until the mixture is syrupy.

3 Add the fruit to the pan and simmer gently over a medium heat for 3–4 minutes until heated through. Add the brandy to the pan and set alight with a match. Shake the pan until the flames die down, then serve at once.

Busy mum's lifesaver Turn this into an autumn dish by using apples and blackberries in place of the red fruit. Cook the apple slices first in a knob of butter until they start turning golden, then add them to the syrup with the blackberries and flame as before.

Lemon and apple steamed sponge pud

My grandmother used to make wonderful old-fashioned puddings for us children and one of my favourites was the one known as 'top hat' sponge pudding – yellowy buttery sponge with a jammy cap on it. This pud is inspired by her.

➡ Serve with clotted cream or pouring cream.

Serves 6
Prepare 20 minutes
Cook 1½ hours

150g (5oz) butter
100g (4oz) light muscovado sugar
1 medium cooking apple, about 200g (7oz), peeled, cored and diced
100g (4oz) caster sugar
grated rind and juice of 2 lemons
2 medium free-range eggs, beaten
175g (6oz) self-raising flour

1 Melt 50g (2oz) of the butter and mix with the muscovado sugar. Stir in the diced apple and set aside.

2 Beat the remaining butter and the caster sugar together in a mixing bowl until pale and light. Beat in the lemon rind then the beaten eggs a little at a time. Sift in the flour and fold into the creamed ingredients with the lemon juice to give a soft consistency.

3 Spoon half the apple mixture into the base of a buttered 1.2 litre (2 pint) pudding basin. Top with half the sponge mixture then add the rest of the apple, followed by the sponge mixture. Level the surface. Cover the basin with greaseproof paper and foil tied tightly with string. Steam in a covered pan for 1½ hours, topping up with boiling water regularly. Turn out on to a warm serving plate.

Busy mum's lifesaver It's worth investing in one of those pudding basins with a fitted plastic lid if you are going to make lots of steamed puds: then you won't have to mess around with paper and string. I also recommend using a steamer as it makes it easier to lift the basin in and out of the pan.

Anna's Swedish rice pudding

My Swedish aunt always serves this indulgent rice pudding on Christmas Eve. It's a world away from traditional nursery rice pudding and is even better made in advance as the flavours develop and mature. ➡ Serve with the mulled wine fruit compote on the opposite page.

Serves 6
Prepare 15 minutes
Cook 35 minutes plus chilling time

600ml (1 pint) full cream milk
1 vanilla pod
100g (4oz) short-grain pudding rice
25g (1oz) caster sugar
150ml (¼ pint) double cream, lightly whipped
50g (2oz) blanched almonds, toasted and roughly chopped
2–3 tbsp spiced rum or cherry brandy (optional)
toasted pine nuts and shreds of lemon peel, to decorate

1 Put the milk in a pan and add the vanilla pod. Bring to the boil and stir in the rice. Simmer for 5 minutes, stirring frequently, then cover and simmer very gently for a further 25 minutes until the mixture is thickened and the rice is tender. Remove the vanilla pod, transfer the rice to a bowl and leave to cool completely, stirring occasionally to prevent a skin forming.

2 Stir the caster sugar into the cool rice and fold in the cream, followed by the almonds and rum or brandy if using. Chill until ready to serve. Spoon into serving glasses or ramekins and decorate with toasted pine nuts and lemon peel.

Mulled wine fruit compote

You can buy useful cartons of ready-prepared mixed frozen fruit, which are ideal for making this compote. The flavour comes from Glogg, a traditional Swedish mulled wine served on Christmas Eve, a perfect occasion for this pud.

➡ Serve with the rice pudding on the opposite page, or try it with thick yogurt and those lovely thin Swedish spice biscuits.

Serves 6
Prepare 5 minutes
Cook 10 minutes plus chilling time

150ml (¼ pint) fruity red wine, such
    as Merlot
50g (2oz) golden granulated sugar
4 cardamom pods, split open
1 cinnamon stick
3–4 cloves
freshly ground nutmeg and black
    pepper
grated rind and juice of 1 orange
450g (1lb) frozen red/black fruit mix
    (a Black Forest fruits mixture is
    ideal)

1 Put the wine in a pan with the sugar, spices, orange rind and juice. Heat gently, stirring, until the sugar dissolves, then bring to the boil and simmer for 2–3 minutes until syrupy.

2 Add the frozen fruit to the syrup, bring to the boil and simmer gently for 5 minutes then spoon into a bowl and leave to cool. Chill before serving.

Baked figs with orange

This is one of the simplest recipes I know and one of the most delicious. It also works well with fresh peaches, apricots, pears, plums and apples. The cream added at the end mixes with the sugary juices to make a wonderful sauce.

Serves 4
Prepare 5 minutes
Cook 30 minutes

8 ripe figs
50g (2oz) unsalted butter, diced
50g (2oz) light muscovado sugar
grated rind and juice of 1 orange
150ml (¼ pint) double cream

1 Preheat the oven to 220°C/fan oven 200°C/Gas Mark 7. Cut the figs in half from stem to base and arrange cut-side up in a single layer in a shallow gratin or baking dish.

2 Scatter the diced butter, sugar and orange rind over the figs and pour over the juice. Bake for 25–30 minutes until tender and lightly browned. Remove the dish from the oven and pour the cream over the fruit. Serve warm or at room temperature.

Banana and strawberry kebabs with Mars bar sauce

As a child, our family Sunday lunches always ended with ice cream topped with a deliciously gooey Mars bar sauce. In the summer I serve the same sauce with these fruit kebabs cooked on the barbecue. They cook almost as well under a hot grill, so you can enjoy them at any time of year and you can vary the fruit according to what you have to hand.

➡ Serve with vanilla ice cream.

Serves 4
Prepare 10 minutes
Cook 10 minutes

25g (1oz) butter
1 tbsp honey
¼ tsp ground cinnamon
3 large ripe bananas
230g (8oz) strawberries

For the sauce
2 large Mars bars, roughly chopped
4–6 tbsp double cream

1 Melt the butter with the honey and cinnamon. Peel the bananas and cut them into thick slices on a slant. Thread the slices on to skewers with the strawberries and brush with the melted butter mixture. Chill until you need them.

2 For the sauce, heat the chopped Mars bars with the cream over a low heat, stirring, until melted. Do not allow to boil. Keep warm.

3 Cook the kebabs on the hot barbecue for 5–8 minutes, turning occasionally and brushing with the butter and honey mixture until the bananas turn golden. Serve the kebabs with the warm Mars bar sauce poured over.

Busy mum's lifesaver You can cook bananas in their skins directly on the barbecue grill, turning them until they are blackened. Then cut the skin open and spoon in honey, rum and cream so that the lucky recipient can scoop out a combination of all the flavours in one go – incredibly simple and completely sublime!

Sticky banana and stem ginger pudding

This is a great way to use up those blackening bananas in the fruit bowl. Banana and ginger transform the already irresistible sticky toffee pudding into food for angels. It's good hot but any leftovers turn into an acceptable (but rather sticky) cake.

⟶ Serve with custard or pouring cream.

Serves 6–8
Prepare 20 minutes
Cook 30 minutes

150g (5oz) unsalted butter
150g (5oz) golden caster sugar
2 medium free-range eggs
230g (8oz) plain flour
1 tsp baking powder
1 tsp ground ginger
2 ripe bananas, mashed
150g (5oz) light muscovado sugar
2 pieces stem ginger, finely chopped
4 tbsp double cream

1 Preheat the oven to 180°C/fan oven 160°C/Gas Mark 4. Beat half the butter with the caster sugar until pale and light, then beat in the eggs one at a time. Sift the flour with the baking powder and ground ginger, and fold into the creamed ingredients with the mashed bananas. Spoon into a buttered 1.75 litre (3 pint) shallow baking dish and level the surface. Cook for 25–30 minutes until well risen and firm to touch.

2 While the pudding is cooking place the remaining butter, muscovado sugar, chopped stem ginger and cream together in a pan. Heat until melted then simmer gently for 3–4 minutes until thick. Set aside. Remove the pudding from the oven and pour over the sauce. Return the dish to the oven for 5 minutes until the top is bubbling and golden.

Fresh raspberry and redcurrant tart

Fresh British raspberries are my favourite soft fruit. At the start of the season all they need is a spoonful of double cream to make them the perfect end to a meal. Later on, use them to make this tart, which is equally delicious warm or cold. For a special occasion you could make little tartlets.

➡️ Serve with extra pouring cream.

Serves 6
Prepare 30 minutes
Cook 45 minutes

175g (6oz) plain flour
75g (3oz) unsalted butter at room
    temperature, diced
50g (2oz) caster sugar
1 large free-range egg, beaten

For the filling
150ml (¼ pint) crème fraîche
125ml (4fl oz) Greek-style yogurt
50g (2oz) caster sugar
2 large free-range eggs
230g (8oz) fresh raspberries
100g (4oz) redcurrants, removed
    from their strings

1 Preheat the oven to 200°C/fan oven 180°C/Gas Mark 6. Sift the flour on to a clean work surface and make a well in the centre. Put the butter, sugar and egg in the well and work together with your fingertips, gradually drawing in the flour to form a stiff dough. Don't overmix. Knead lightly until smooth, then wrap and chill for 30 minutes. (You can mix up all the ingredients in a processor but don't overprocess – stop as soon as the pastry starts to come together.)

2 Roll out the pastry and use it to line a 25cm (10in) loose-bottomed flan tin. Line the pastry with crumpled greaseproof paper and fill with baking beans. Bake for 10 minutes, then remove the beans and paper.

3 Beat together the crème fraîche, yogurt, sugar and eggs. Arrange the raspberries and redcurrants over the base of the pastry case and pour over the cream and egg mixture. Reduce the oven temperature to 180°C/ fan oven 160°C/Gas Mark 4. Bake the tart for 35–40 minutes until the filling is set and golden. Leave to cool on a wire rack. Chill in the tin until ready to serve.

Busy mum's lifesaver Despite cheating and buying readymade pastry quite often these days, I really think it's worth making sweet pastry for this tart as the flavour will be noticeably better. It's such a simple dessert that you need the buttery sweetness of homemade pastry. Only use readymade if you can find sweet shortcrust made with butter, which is not as widely available as some of the other pastries. Use other fruit in season – plums, apricots, cherries, peaches, pears or apples.

bake me a cake

You can tell I'm definitely of the 'live to eat' sisterhood rather than the 'eat to live' crew. Food is one of the main pleasures of life, and cakes and biscuits are far too delicious to put in room 101. Home baking is one of the things that makes life a joy; the process itself is satisfying and the results bring people together. A slice of cake or a homemade cookie is the real deal, whatever advertisers tell us. Take some time to make these recipes with your children, even if it is only once in a blue moon. They will remember the experience and you'll enjoy the time you spend together . Some of the recipes, such as the hazelnut and lemon biscotti on page 184, make lovely homemade presents. ⟶

Irish coffee layer cake

This spectacular cake works as a dessert, morning-coffee treat or tea-time centrepiece. I came up with the recipe for St Patrick's Day – as I'm a huge fan of Irish coffee and coffee cake, it seemed obvious to combine the two.

Makes one 20cm (8in) cake
Prepare 30 minutes
Cook 30 minutes

230g (8oz) butter
230g (8oz) golden caster sugar
4 medium free-range eggs, beaten
2 tbsp instant coffee granules
230g (8oz) self-raising flour, sifted
2 tbsp Irish whiskey

For the filling and topping
25g (1oz) butter
250g pot mascarpone
175g (6oz) icing sugar, sifted
1 tsp instant coffee granules
1 tbsp Irish whiskey
chocolate coffee beans, to decorate

1 Preheat the oven to 180°C/fan oven 160°C/Gas Mark 4. Butter and base-line two 20cm (8in) sandwich tins with baking parchment. Beat the butter with the sugar until pale and light. Beat in the eggs a little at a time. Mix the coffee with 2 tablespoons boiling water. Fold the flour into the cake mixture followed by the coffee and whiskey.

2 Spoon into the tins and level the surface. Bake for 30 minutes until well risen and firm to touch. Rest in the tins for a couple of minutes then turn on to wire racks to cool completely.

3 For the filling beat the butter with 25g (1oz) of the mascarpone then beat in all of the icing sugar apart from 2 tablespoons, until very pale and light. Mix the coffee granules with a teaspoon of boiling water and then beat into the icing. Gradually beat in the whiskey. Sandwich the cakes together with the buttercream.

4 Beat the remaining mascarpone with the reserved icing sugar and spread over the top of the cake. Decorate with chocolate coffee beans.

Busy mum's lifesaver Given the chance, this cake gets better after a couple of days: if possible, make it in advance and store in an airtight tin.

Chunky chocolate biscuit cake

This recipe shows perfectly the pitfalls that lie in wait for vegetarians. Despite having edited a veggie magazine for nearly five years I made a silly mistake for the photography and put mini marshmallows on top of the biscuit cake. It was only when a colleague reminded me that marshmallows contain gelatine that I realised what I'd done. Instead of reshooting we decided to leave the shot as is, as a warning to you all – always read the label. Sometimes the most innocent-seeming foods have hidden ingredients. Luckily the marshmallows are not essential to success – the dried fruit is far more important.

Makes 24 squares
Prepare 5 minutes
Cook 5 minutes

100g (4oz) butter, cubed

2 tbsp golden syrup

150g (5oz) dark chocolate, broken
  into chunks

200g (7oz) rich tea or digestive
  biscuits, crushed

100g (4oz) dried fruit mix, plus extra
  for scattering

25g (1oz) nibbed almonds

200g (7oz) milk chocolate, broken
  into chunks

1 Place the butter, golden syrup and dark chocolate in a small pan (or the microwave) and heat very gently until melted. Place the biscuits in a bowl with the dried fruit and almonds. Pour over the melted ingredients and mix thoroughly. Spoon into a greased and base-lined 30 x 20cm (12 x 8in) shallow cake tin and press level with the back of a spoon. Chill for 15–20 minutes until set.

2 Melt the milk chocolate in the microwave or in a small bowl set over a pan of simmering water and spread over the top of the biscuit cake. Scatter with the dried fruit (and marshmallows if using) and press into the chocolate then chill again until set. Cut into squares and store in an airtight tin.

Lemon, white chocolate and pistachio butterfly cakes

Pretty as a picture and a flavour combination made in heaven. The lemon balances the sweetness of the white chocolate while the pistachio adds fresh colour and flavour. I remember the magic as a child making butterfly cakes. Baking these little cakes with your children will doubtless bring back memories for you – and build new ones for your children.

Makes 12
Prepare 15 minutes
Cook 15 minutes

100g (4oz) butter
100g (4oz) golden caster sugar
grated rind of 1 lemon
2 medium free-range eggs, beaten
100g (4oz) self-raising flour
½ tsp baking powder
2 tbsp lemon juice

For the icing
50g (2oz) white chocolate
25g (1oz) butter
100g (4oz) icing sugar, sifted
25g (1oz) pistachio nuts, chopped
icing sugar, for dusting

1 Preheat the oven to 180°C/ fan oven 160°C/Gas Mark 4. Arrange 12 paper cases in bun tins. Cream the butter and sugar together in a mixing bowl with the lemon rind until very light and fluffy. Add the eggs a little at a time, beating each addition well.

2 Sift the flour with the baking powder and carefully fold in with the lemon juice to give the mixture a soft dropping consistency. Divide between the cases and level the tops. Bake for 12–15 minutes until well risen and a skewer pushed into one of the cakes emerges clean. Cool on wire racks.

3 To make the icing, melt the chocolate in a small bowl over a pan of simmering water or in the microwave. Cool for 5 minutes then beat into the butter. Gradually beat in the icing sugar. Slice a little circle off the top of each cake and cut it in half. Spread the cut surface with icing and arrange the cut halves to look like butterfly wings. Scatter over the pistachio nuts and dust with icing sugar.

Banana and cardamom tea loaf

There always seems to be a banana or two going black in the fruit bowl – what better excuse to bake this tea loaf. It's extremely popular with my yoga group and is really good for packed lunches.

Makes 1 loaf
Prepare 15 minutes
Cook 1 hour

1 green tea bag
100g (4oz) dried cranberries
230g (8oz) self-raising flour
1 tsp baking powder
1 tbsp cardamom pods
50g (2oz) butter, cubed
100g (4oz) demerara sugar
grated rind of 1 orange
5 tbsp spiced rum
1 medium free-range egg, beaten
2 ripe bananas, mashed

1 Preheat the oven to 180°C/fan oven 160°C/Gas Mark 4. Butter and base-line a 1.75 litre (3 pint) loaf tin. Pour 150ml (¼ pint) boiling water over the tea bag and add the cranberries. Leave to steep for 5 minutes then remove the tea bag.

2 Sift the flour and baking powder into a mixing bowl. Lightly crush the cardamom pods and remove the seeds. Add the seeds to the flour then rub in the butter till the mixture looks like fine breadcrumbs. Stir in the demerara sugar, orange rind and rum.

3 Whisk the egg with the tea and cranberries and add to the dry ingredients with the mashed bananas. Mix well then spoon into the prepared tin and level the surface. Bake for 50–60 minutes until well risen, golden and firm to touch. Turn out, remove the lining paper and cool on a wire rack. Wrap and keep for 24 hours to allow the flavours to develop, then serve sliced.

Busy mum's lifesaver If making the tea loaf for small children substitute orange juice instead of spiced rum – use the fresh juice from the orange that you grated for its rind.

Hazelnut and lemon biscotti

In Italy these little biscotti are served at the end of a meal with a glass of Vin Santo, a fortified dessert wine. They are available in Italian delicatessens but are very simple to make at home. My recipe uses hazelnuts – the biscuits taste wonderful with ice creams and fruit fools or dunked in a cappuccino.

Makes 10
Prepare 5 minutes
Cook 35 minutes

100g (4oz) plain flour
¼ teaspoon baking powder
75g (3oz) caster sugar
75g (3oz) toasted hazelnuts, roughly chopped
grated rind of ½ lemon
1 medium free-range egg, beaten

1 Preheat the oven to 200°C/fan oven 180°C/Gas Mark 6. Sift the flour and baking powder into a bowl and stir in the sugar, hazelnuts and lemon rind. Work in the egg to give a firm dough.

2 Turn the dough on to a lightly floured work surface and roll into a long sausage about 23cm (9in) long. Transfer to a baking sheet lined with baking parchment and bake for about 25 minutes until pale golden.

3 Remove the baking sheet from the oven and, working carefully, cut the biscuit mixture on the diagonal into 10 pieces. Arrange the biscuits cut-side down back on the baking sheet and return to the oven for a further 10 minutes until golden and firm. Transfer to a wire rack to cool. Store in an airtight container for up to 10 days.

Busy mum's lifesaver You can add all kinds of flavourings to these biscuits: try pistachio and orange or rosemary and almond, or chocolate chips. Pack them in Kilner jars for a foodie Christmas gift.

Plum and hazelnut upside-down cake

Bakes that work both as puddings or sliced and served as cake are incredibly useful and this is a perfect example. I make it for Sunday lunch while listening to *The Archers* and serve it with custard, then any leftovers go into a tin for the week ahead.

Makes one 20cm (8in) cake
Prepare 20 minutes
Cook 50 minutes

150g (5oz) butter
50g (2oz) light muscovado sugar
50g (2oz) roasted chopped hazelnuts
1 tsp ground cinnamon
6 ripe plums, stoned and halved
75g (3oz) golden caster sugar
grated rind of 1 orange
1 large free-range egg, beaten
150g (5oz) self-raising flour
½ tsp bicarbonate of soda
100ml (4fl oz) soured cream

1 Preheat the oven to 180°C/fan oven 160°C/Gas Mark 4. Butter and base-line a deep round 20cm (8in) cake tin. Melt 75g (3oz) of the butter and mix with the muscovado sugar, hazelnuts and cinnamon. Scatter over the base of the cake tin and press the halved plums into the sugar mix, cut-side down.

2 Beat the remaining butter with the caster sugar and orange rind until pale and creamy then beat in the egg a little at a time. Sift the flour with the bicarbonate of soda and fold into the creamed mixture with the soured cream to give a soft consistency. Spoon on top of the plums and level the surface.

3 Bake for 45–50 minutes until well risen, golden and firm to touch. Cool in the tin for 15 minutes then turn on to a wire rack. Serve warm with cream or cold. Store in an airtight container.

Busy mum's lifesaver This cake works with all kinds of fruit: try peaches, apricots, apples or pears. It's a great way to use up what's left in the fruit bowl and the cooked cake also freezes successfully. Defrost overnight in a cool place, keeping the cake loosely covered.

Goat's cheese and chive scones

I serve these savoury scones with soup or salads, or make mini ones for nibbles to hand round before a meal, topping them with dollops of mascarpone and strips of barbecued vegetables tossed with a little balsamic vinegar – they're ideal for packed lunches too. Use a firm, crumbly goat's cheese to make the dough, rather than any of the soft fresh types.

Makes 10–12 scones
Prepare 10 minutes
Cook 15 minutes

230g (8oz) self-raising flour
pinch of salt
large pinch of cayenne pepper
½ teaspoon baking powder
25g (1oz) butter, diced
2 tbsp snipped fresh chives
50g (2oz) firm goat's cheese, crumbled
150ml (5fl oz) natural yogurt
beaten egg, to glaze

1 Preheat the oven to 220°C/fan oven 200°C/Gas Mark 7. Place a baking sheet in the oven to heat. Sift the flour, salt, cayenne and baking powder into a large mixing bowl. Rub the butter into the dry ingredients until the mixture resembles fine breadcrumbs. Stir in the chives and goat's cheese. Add the yogurt and mix to a soft dough with the blade of a knife.

2 Turn the dough on to a floured work surface and knead lightly. Roll out to 2.5cm (1in) thick and use a plain 5cm (2in) cutter to cut out rounds. Roll out the trimmings and cut more scones. Place on the hot baking sheet and brush the tops with beaten egg. Bake for 12–15 minutes, until well risen and golden. Transfer to a wire rack to cool.

Busy mum's lifesaver **Try alternative flavourings, such as basil and feta, or sun-dried tomato, black olive and Parmesan.**

Sun-dried tomato soda bread

Soda bread is so quick and easy to make – great in an emergency. You might have noticed I've used a lot of sun-dried tomato paste in this book. Since its introduction it's become a real standby in my kitchen. It's not as sharp as tomato purée as it's preserved with oil, and it adds real depth of flavour.

Makes 1 loaf
Prepare 15 minutes
Cook 45 minutes

400g (14oz) plain white flour
400g (14oz) stoneground wholemeal flour
2 tsp bicarbonate of soda
1 tsp salt
300ml (½ pint) semi-skimmed milk
250ml (8fl oz) natural yogurt
2 tbsp sun-dried tomato paste

1 Preheat the oven to 220°C/fan oven 200°C/Gas Mark 7. Sift the flours with the bicarbonate of soda and salt into a large mixing bowl. Whisk together the milk and yogurt and stir into the dry ingredients with the tomato paste. Mix to a soft dough, but don't overmix – you want swirls of colour through the bread. Turn the dough on to a lightly floured work surface and knead lightly to form a rough circle about 6cm (2½in) thick.

2 Transfer to a lightly floured baking sheet and mark a deep cross on the top with the handle of a wooden spoon. Dust the top with a little extra plain flour if desired. Bake for 20–25 minutes until risen, then reduce the oven temperature to 200°C/fan oven 180°C/Gas Mark 6 and bake for a further 20 minutes until golden and the base of the loaf sounds hollow when tapped. Cool on a wire rack.

Busy mum's lifesaver For a chive and cheese loaf, leave out the tomato paste and substitute 4 tbsp snipped fresh chives and 75g (3oz) crumbled hard cheese such as a crumbly Wensleydale. It's wonderful toasted with grilled cheese.

Ginger crunchies

Here is my favourite biscuit recipe based on one of my grandmother's – they're called crunchies but are actually softer than the classic gingernut and more melting in texture. There's nothing better to dunk in your tea or to enjoy with a glass of milk.

Makes 30
Prepare 15 minutes
Cook 18 minutes

230g (8oz) plain flour
1 tsp baking powder
½ tsp bicarbonate of soda
3 tsp ground ginger
100g (4oz) butter, cubed
150g (5oz) demerara sugar
3 pieces stem ginger, finely chopped
1 large free-range egg
2 tbsp golden syrup

1 Preheat the oven to 180°C/fan oven 160°C/Gas Mark 4. Sift the flour, baking powder, bicarbonate of soda and ground ginger into a large mixing bowl. Rub in the butter until the mixture resembles fine breadcrumbs, then stir in the sugar and stem ginger. Mix together the egg and golden syrup with a fork and add to the dried ingredients. Mix to a stiff dough with a wooden spoon.

2 Roll the mixture into walnut sized balls and place on greased baking sheets with room to spread. Press down with a fork and bake for 15–18 minutes until golden. Leave on the tray for 5 minutes then transfer to a wire rack to cool. Store in an airtight container.

Marmalade spice cake

This is another of those cakes that tastes delicious freshly baked but goes on improving if you get the chance to store it for a few days. Use a good-quality shop-bought marmalade for the best flavour – I can never bring myself to use my precious homemade marmalade unless I've made far too much.

Makes one 23cm (9in) cake
Prepare 20 minutes
Cook 1 hour

175g (6oz) butter
150g (5oz) golden caster sugar
2 tbsp golden syrup
2 large free-range eggs, beaten
10 tbsp orange marmalade
350g (12oz) self-raising flour
1 tsp baking powder
1 tsp each ground cinnamon and
　　ground nutmeg
150ml (¼ pint) semi-skimmed milk,
　　plus 2 tbsp
100g (4oz) icing sugar, sifted

1 Preheat the oven to 180°C/ fan oven 160°C/Gas Mark 4. Butter and base-line a deep round 23cm (9in) cake tin. Cream the butter with the caster sugar until pale and light then beat in the golden syrup followed by the eggs a little at a time. Stir in half the marmalade.

2 Sift the flour with the baking powder and spices and fold half into the creamed ingredients. Stir in 150ml (¼ pint) of the milk then the remaining flour to give a stiff creamed mixture. Spoon into the prepared tin and smooth the surface. Bake for 55–60 minutes until golden and well risen. A skewer should emerge dry from the middle of the cake. Turn on to a wire rack and leave to cool, base upwards.

3 When the cake is cool, heat the remaining marmalade in a small pan until warmed through then spread over the cake. Mix the sifted icing sugar with the remaining milk to give a thin icing. Drizzle over the cake, letting the icing drizzle down the sides. Leave to set.

finishing touches

Good gravy, a zingy salsa or homemade ketchup – for the veggie cook, these are like the designer accessories of the fashion world. Used well, they have the power to bring a meal together and transform a well-meaning but maybe standard dish into something out of the ordinary. They bring flavours into balance, add welcome succulence to drier recipes and extra punch to everyday offerings. Keep them on standby and boost your reputation as an inspired cook. ⟶

Pine nut and Parmesan dressing

Essentially a simple pesto, this recipe is really good with salad leaves, griddled or barbecued Mediterranean vegetables, such as strips of courgette and peppers, or steamed asparagus. I also use it tossed with freshly cooked new potatoes for a superb salad.

Prepare 5 minutes

25g (1oz) pine nuts
1 clove garlic, peeled
a little rock salt
4 tbsp freshly grated Parmesan
2 tbsp chopped fresh flat-leaf parsley
4 tbsp extra-virgin olive oil
freshly ground black pepper

1 Place the pine nuts and garlic in a mortar with a sprinkling of rock salt. Use a pestle to pound the ingredients together until you have a smooth paste. Then work in the Parmesan and parsley. Gradually add the olive oil a little at a time until you have a thick dressing. Check the seasoning, adding freshly ground black pepper to taste.

Busy mum's lifesaver Make up a batch and store in a screw-topped jar in the fridge for up to three days.

Rich onion gravy

One of the challenges for veggies is to come up with a flavourful alternative to meaty gravies. Roast veg such as the recipe on page 20 cry out for good gravy. Now that you can buy top-quality fresh vegetable stock from the chiller cabinet at the supermarket, this recipe does the trick. Don't let the onions burn or they will go bitter and ruin the flavour – you need rich golden onions that are not at all black.

Makes 600ml (1 pint)
Prepare 10 minutes
Cook 20 minutes

2 large onions, sliced
1 tbsp olive oil
2 tbsp plain flour
600ml (1 pint) vegetable stock
½ teaspoon sun-dried tomato paste
1 tsp red wine vinegar or balsamic
   vinegar
1 tbsp chopped fresh thyme
salt and freshly ground black pepper

1 Put the onions in a frying pan with the oil and cook really gently for 15 minutes, stirring occasionally, until very soft but not at all coloured. Raise the heat, sprinkle with a little salt and cook for a further 5 minutes until a rich golden colour.

2 Stir in the flour and cook for 1 minute, then gradually add the stock, tomato paste, vinegar and thyme. Bring to the boil, stirring, and simmer for 3–4 minutes to cook out the flour. Season to taste and serve. If you prefer a smooth gravy, purée it in a blender, but I rather like the oniony bits.

Cucumber and walnut raita

A yogurt-based raita is the perfect accompaniment for more fiery spiced dishes or roasted root vegetables, which can be a little dry. I always serve it with the chickpea curry on page 30.

Serves 4
Prepare 10 minutes

¼ small cucumber
200g (7oz) natural yogurt
25g (1oz) walnut pieces, finely
   chopped
1 tsp cumin seeds
few drops Tabasco sauce
2 tbsp lemon juice
3 tbsp chopped fresh coriander or
   mint
salt and freshly ground black pepper

1 Grate the cucumber on a coarse grater and squeeze in kitchen paper to remove excess liquid. Place the yogurt in a mixing bowl and stir in the cucumber and walnuts.

2 Dry-fry the cumin seeds for 30 seconds in a small frying pan, then grind to a powder in a pestle and mortar or small processor or spice mill. Add to the yogurt with the Tabasco, lemon juice, coriander or mint and seasoning. Cover and chill until needed.

Busy mum's lifesaver Leave out the cumin, Tabasco and salt, add a little sugar and you've got a topping for cooked fruit – try it with barbecued pineapple slices or peach halves.

Lemon and walnut salsa verde

Parsley and garlic are the essential ingredients for the simplest and one of the most useful recipes in the book. I grow both in my garden and the flavour is outstanding but I also make it all year round with supermarket ingredients as it's so good. Make it with your very best extra-virgin olive oil. Use the sauce as a marinade or to brush over practically any vegetables before you roast or barbecue them, and spread it over toasted bread for the simplest and best bruschetta.

Serves 4
Prepare 5 minutes

1–2 cloves garlic
1 tbsp capers
50g (2oz) walnut pieces
6 tbsp chopped fresh flat-leaf parsley
grated rind and juice of 1 lemon
4 tbsp extra-virgin olive oil
salt and freshly ground black pepper

1 Finely chop the garlic, capers and walnuts by hand for the best texture – you can do it in a blender, but just take care not to overprocess. Place in a small bowl and stir in the parsley, lemon rind and juice, oil and plenty of seasoning.

Busy mum's lifesaver The salsa verde will store in a covered container in the fridge for up to 48 hours. For non-veggies it goes really well with all kinds of grilled meat and fish but is particularly good with salmon and lamb.

Fresh mango and coconut chutney

This sweet and sour chutney adds a lovely fresh flavour to vegetable curries and dishes such as the koftas on page 76.

Serves 4
Prepare 10 minutes

1 green chilli, deseeded and roughly
    chopped
4 tbsp desiccated coconut
4 tbsp chopped fresh coriander
2 tsp chopped fresh root ginger
1 clove garlic, roughly chopped
juice of ½ lime
1 medium ripe mango
salt

1 Place the chilli in a food processor and add the coconut, coriander, ginger, garlic and lime juice. Blend to a smooth paste, then add salt to taste.

2 Peel the mango. Cut the flesh away from the stone. Cut it into small cubes and place in a serving bowl. Pour the coconut mixture over the mango and mix well. Cover and chill until needed.

Busy mum's lifesaver Try adding a diced avocado too.

Quick lemon hollandaise

I never seem to have time to stand whisking hot butter into egg yolks to make a proper hollandaise sauce as I was taught at Leith's cookery school. This version is made with a handheld blender and it's a pretty good substitute. It's delicious with asparagus and a Michelin-starred chef friend always serves it with broccoli. It makes a starter or veg accompaniment really special.

Serves 4–6
Prepare 10 minutes
Cook 3 minutes

3 tbsp white wine vinegar
2 tsp chopped fresh tarragon
6 black peppercorns
1 shallot, finely chopped
3 large free-range egg yolks
100g (4oz) unsalted butter
grated rind and juice of ½ lemon
salt and freshly ground black pepper

1 Place the vinegar in a small pan with the tarragon, peppercorns and shallot. Bring to the boil and cook until the vinegar is reduced to 1 tablespoon. Strain and leave to cool.

2 Place the reduced vinegar in a basin with the egg yolks and mix with a handheld blender. Heat the butter in a small pan until really bubbling but not browned. Hold the blender running with one hand and pour the hot butter on the egg yolks in a steady stream. The sauce should be thick and creamy. Stir in the lemon rind and juice, season to taste and serve immediately.

Busy mum's lifesaver To make the quick hollandaise in a worktop blender use one whole egg and two yolks to give enough volume for the machine to work properly.

Romesco sauce

This simple sauce comes from the Tarragona region in Spain where it is traditionally served with barbecued shellfish but it's just as good as a dip with crudités or with the barbecued asparagus on page 72 or with pasta. Grill the onions, peppers and tomatoes over the barbecue for the best smoky flavour.

Serves 4
Prepare 10 minutes
Cook 15 minutes

1 medium onion, peeled
3–4 cloves garlic
2 red peppers
6–8 Italian vine tomatoes
50g (2oz) blanched almonds or
   hazelnuts
1 large red chilli, deseeded and
   chopped
2 tbsp red wine vinegar
100ml (4fl oz) extra-virgin olive oil
salt and freshly ground black pepper

1 Preheat the barbecue or grill. Halve the onion horizontally. Thread the cloves of garlic on to a wooden skewer. Place the onion, garlic, whole peppers and tomatoes on the hot barbecue or under the grill and cook for 8–15 minutes, turning regularly, until the skins are charred. The garlic and tomatoes will cook faster.

2 Place the peppers and tomatoes in a bowl, cover and set aside for 5 minutes until their skins have loosened. Peel and deseed, catching any juice. Roughly chop the flesh and place in a blender with the juice.

3 Dry-fry the nuts in a small frying pan for about 2 minutes, until golden. Add to the tomato mixture and process to a coarse paste. Squeeze the garlic out and add to the blender with the onion and chilli. With the motor running, slowly pour in the vinegar and olive oil, then continue to process until the sauce is smooth. Season to taste. Serve at room temperature for the best flavour.

Busy mum's lifesaver Store any extra sauce in a covered container in the fridge for up to a week. Bring the sauce to room temperature before serving, to allow the flavours to develop.

Fresh tomato chilli ketchup

This smooth sauce is almost jammy and a lovely alternative to bought ketchup; brush it over vegetables as they cook on the barbecue, or serve a little of the sauce with kebabs or char-grilled root vegetables. Use fresh tomatoes only if they are really full of flavour, otherwise used canned Italian plum tomatoes for the correct intensity.

Serves 4–6
Prepare 5 minutes
Cook 25 minutes

750g (1¾lb) ripe plum tomatoes or
    2 x 400g cans Italian tomatoes,
    drained
2 mild red chillies, deseeded and
    roughly chopped (use hot chillies if
    you prefer a fiery taste)
3 cloves garlic, roughly chopped
50g (2oz) light muscovado sugar
1 tbsp red wine vinegar
4 tbsp chopped fresh basil
salt

1 If using fresh tomatoes, chop them roughly. Process the tomatoes with the chillies and garlic in a blender or food processor until smooth. Sieve the mixture into a saucepan, pressing through as much as you can.

2 Stir in the sugar and vinegar and cook over a gentle heat until the sugar dissolves, then bring the relish to the boil and simmer for 20–25 minutes until thickened. Stir in the basil and salt to taste. Serve hot or cold.

Busy mum's lifesaver Pour the ketchup into warmed pots as soon as it is removed from the heat and cover immediately with airtight lids. Store in the fridge for up to 1 month. I like to make it in small Kilner jars and give to friends for Christmas presents. Or make a really big batch and freeze it in ice cube trays to add individual portions to pasta sauces or stews.

Oven-baked honey muesli

I like to make my own muesli – then I know what's gone into it. It also means you can vary the fruit, nuts and seeds, depending on what's in the cupboard or is about to go past its use-by date. This recipe came from a great friend of my mother's back in the days when we were only just discovering muesli, let alone the joys of granola. Serve with fresh fruit and yogurt or with fruit compote in winter – it makes a really good snack as well as a delicious breakfast.

Serves 6
Prepare 10 minutes
Cook 50 minutes

200g (7oz) organic jumbo oats
50g (2oz) mixed seeds
75g (3oz) dried fruit or berry mix
50g (2oz) chopped mixed nuts
50g (2oz) desiccated coconut
50ml (2fl oz) sunflower oil
150g (5oz) clear honey

I Preheat the oven to 160°C/fan oven 140°C/Gas Mark 2. Mix together the oats, seeds, fruit, nuts and coconut. Warm the oil and honey together in a small pan until blended, then pour over the dry ingredients and mix well. Spread over the base of a large roasting tin in a thin layer and bake for 45–50 minutes, stirring occasionally until crisp and pale golden. Leave to cool. Store in an airtight container.

index

Note: Page numbers in **bold** denote major sections.

conversion tables

The tables below are approximate and are intended as a guide only

EUROPEAN/AMERICAN CONVERSIONS

	Metric	Imperial	USA
brown sugar	175g	6oz	1 cup
butter	100g	4oz	1 stick
butter	230g	8oz	1 cup
caster and granulated sugar	25g	1oz	2 level tbsp
caster and granulated sugar	230g	8oz	1 cup
flour	150g	5oz	1 cup
dried fruit	200g	7oz	1 cup
rice	200g	7oz	1 cup
grated Parmesan	100g	4oz	1 cup
fresh breadcrumbs	50g	2oz	1 cup

LIQUIDS

Metric	Imperial UK	USA
5ml	1 tsp	1 tsp
15ml	1 tbsp	½ fl oz
50ml	4 tbsp	¼ cup
150ml	¼ pint	½ cup plus 2 tbsp
300ml	½ pint	1 ¼ cups
600ml	1 pint	2 ½ cups
1.2 litres	2 pints	5 cups

(NB UK and US pints are not equivalent. 1 UK pint = 20floz; 1 US pint = 16floz)

OVEN TEMPERATURES

USA	°C	fan°C	°F	Gas Mark
Very cool	100	80	225	¼
Slow	150	130	275	2
Moderate	170	150	325	3
Moderate	180	160	350	4
Moderately hot	190	170	375	5
Fairly hot	200	180	400	6
Hot	220	200	425	7
Very hot	230	210	445	8